AL BERNSTEIN

30 Years,
30 Undeniable Truths
about Boxing, Sports, and TV

AL BERNSTEIN

30 Years,
30 Undeniable Truths
about Boxing, Sports, and TV

Al Bernstein

DIVERSIONBOOKS

DIVERSION BOOKS

A Division of Diversion Publishing Corp.
80 Fifth Avenue, Suite 1101
New York, New York 10011

www.DiversionBooks.com

For more information, email info@diversionbooks.com.

First Diversion Books edition June 2012.
ISBN: 978-1-938120-30-5

Cover image courtesy of Tom Casino/SHOWTIME

CONTENTS

FOREWORD

By George Foreman

When I think of Al Bernstein and his career, there's one word that comes to mind—growth. In all these years he has always continued to grow. He's always doing something new, and challenging himself to be better. I admire that and it's the reason I am so proud of his career.

I've seen Al do well in so many situations. He is one of the best at taking the past in boxing and bringing it to life. I remember the shows he did with the ESPN Classic called *Big Fights Boxing Hour*. He looked so at home in that boxing library room and he would just make us feel like we were going back in time to relive those great memories. That was Al, "the Boxing Historian."

Then there's the Al everybody knows, who announces fights with so much knowledge and excitement—he treats the fighters with respect and still tells the fans what they need to know. He announced some of my fights, and I always loved when he was going to be one of the commentators. I also had the pleasure of working with Al as a commentator myself. In that role he's grown as well, always working to improve—he's not content to rest on his laurels.

But the real shocker to me was when I saw him take the risk of stepping out there in front of live audiences. At Caesars Palace in Las Vegas he had a show where he introduced boxing video, interviewed celebrities, answered questions from the audience, and just entertained people. And, he *sang*. That's right; Al is a really good singer. I was his guest on one of those shows—we just had the best time and I could see how the people loved seeing Al do something so different. I couldn't believe how he was willing to stand there alone and do that. It's scary to step out and do that. Most people don't take those risks.

Yep, my friend Al Bernstein is always growing, and that's the best compliment I can pay anyone. And now, here he is doing it again with this book. I love that this book shows another side of Al—the funny side that I saw when he was on stage at Caesars Palace. You'll enjoy the stories about boxing, Las Vegas, ESPN, Showtime, and all the interesting people Al has known and covered over the years. He tells these tales with a lot of humor and feeling.

How about this—Al even became a cowboy! I love riding horses down in Texas and, guess what, Al loves it too. He got on a horse for the first time at age thirty, and instead of just riding trails and having fun, of course, Al challenged himself—he competed in celebrity rodeos. You can read about that in this book too.

So enjoy the book. It's sure to entertain you. And then, we'll all just wait to see what Al decides to do next. I guarantee you there will be something new, because that's just Al Bernstein.

INTRODUCTION

Many people will tell you that the hardest part of writing a book is coming up with the right concept and title. Then, they say, the book pretty much writes itself. Of course, most of the people who say that have never written a book.

In truth, even after you get the concept and title you do have to actually write the book—unless you have a ghostwriter. In that case you let him or her interview you for weeks while you sip cocktails at poolside. Then you wait for about four months, and when the ghostwriter delivers the finished manuscript, you become an author. The more you drink, the more colorful the stories are and the better an author you become. Some people drink so much they practically become as good as John Updike.

I would have used the ghostwriter/cocktail-sipping approach to this book if it weren't for one thing . . . guilt. You see, I spent the first ten years of my working life as a newspaperman, and over the last thirty years in broadcasting I have written radio and television scripts, Internet and newspaper columns, magazine articles, and just about anything else you can write. So, with a last name of Bernstein, I think you can see how I might feel a little guilty about farming out the writing of this book to someone else. Inside my head I hear the voice of my late mother saying to me, "I sent you to college to be a writer and this is *your* book. Don't you think *you* should write it? But, I can't tell you what to do . . . do what you want." Imagined guilt from a Jewish mother reaching out from the grave. Case closed—no ghostwriter.

So, not only did I have to write this book, but by doing it myself

I lose the advantage of "deniability" if some of my recollections are wrong. With a ghostwriter you can actually say you were misquoted in your own memoirs. I believe Charles Barkley took that approach.

Don't get me wrong on that title and concept thing. They *are* important. Many literary efforts have been scuttled by titles that just didn't work—like these:

Flying Under the Radar
By Rex Ryan

Eat, Love, Stay
By Kim Kardashian

Abstinence Makes the Heart Grow Fonder
By Tiger Woods

See, it can be tricky. I will admit that I struggled a bit to come up with the right concept and title for this book. Then, I asked myself, "Have I learned any undeniable truths during my career in broadcasting, and would any of those truths be useful to impart in this book?" I answered both those questions with a resounding YES! In fact it was so resounding that it scared Antonio Tarver, who I was having lunch with at the time. So, I came up with the thirty undeniable truths that I have learned over my thirty-year career. Even I was struck by the coincidence that those two numbers happened to match perfectly. Go figure.

Because my undeniable truths are filled with wisdom and even pathos, some may see this book as much more than a breezy and amusing read about sports and television. Some people may see it as a guide map through life—a powerful tool to point them toward a fulfilling existence. Those people would be pretty stupid, but that viewpoint would technically make this a motivational book, and I'm told those sell really well. So, I'm good with that.

Still others may see this book more as a salacious tell-all that leaves you gasping after every page. For instance, you may be surprised to know that in the early 1990s I had an acrimonious breakup with Kirstie Alley after a tumultuous affair. Actually, it would surprise me too. It's not true. And, to be honest, the book isn't really very salacious.

However you perceive this book, I hope you enjoy it. If you do, please tell all your friends how much you like it. If you don't, well, fair is fair—tell them you didn't like it. But, in that case, be sure to mention that it was written by Larry Merchant.

AL BERNSTEIN

30 Years,
30 Undeniable Truths
about Boxing, Sports, and TV

There Is Always Time for Humor

ESPN was not always the sports media empire of gigantic proportions we know today. It did not always have five television networks, a massive radio network, a national magazine, a Website that gets millions of hits, and a themed restaurant.

In 1980, ESPN was one lonely struggling cable network in its first (and some thought last) year of existence that reached only about three million homes in America. I had just joined ESPN as a boxing commentator on the *Top Rank Boxing* series and became one of the merry band of pioneers inventing cable television as we went along. After all, there had never been a twenty-four-hour all-sports television network before, and all of cable television programming represented one big crapshoot.

After a quarter century of existence, the ESPN holiday party had reached the point where it had an employee guest list that topped six thousand people and was held at a massive banquet location that featured several buildings to accommodate the throng. However, at the 1981 ESPN holiday party there were about two hundred people on hand at the glamorous Holiday Inn in Plainville, Connecticut. At the end of the evening Dick Vitale and I were designated to pick out the winning raffle tickets for two lucky ESPN employees. What were those big prizes? They were two twenty-four-inch black and white televisions. I kid you not.

The ESPN programming schedule back then was nothing like the current model. That schedule did not have the NFL, NBA, MLB, and major golf and tennis tourneys that now dot the ESPN schedule. No, back then it was monster truck races, tape-delayed college football and basketball from the lowest conferences, kickboxing, and any other cheaply acquired programming they could get their hands on for about $4.95—give or take a few cents.

The network was certainly in its embryonic stages back then, but the show I was lucky enough to be on, *Top Rank Boxing*, was by far ESPN's most-watched series. How many people were watching? Well, the figure was probably somewhere between the number of children Evander Holyfield has fathered out of wedlock and the number of lawsuits annually filed against Don King—in other words, a big number, but not big by television standards. So, we knew *somebody* was watching and we had to get on the air. That was not always an easy task.

Back then ESPN was to television what M*A*S*H units are to hospitals. In the case of ESPN, however, only shows and careers died from our on-the-air meatball surgery. No people actually perished . . .

In the early days of ESPN, I worked with Sal Marchiano (right) and, on this show, Lightweight Champ Sean O'Grady joined us on the telecast. Back then the ESPN logo looked different, and I did too.

to my knowledge. The budgets were too low and number of shows to do too high. In contrast, on the over-the-air networks—ABC, NBC, and CBS—the 1980s were halcyon days for sports programming. The sports department budgets at those networks rivaled the gross national product of Peru. I think more money was spent at ABC for the creature comforts of Howard Cosell and Director Chet Forte on one Monday night football show than ESPN spent on televising an entire boxing show. I know you think I'm exaggerating, but that's only because you don't know how much money was needed for the creature comforts of Howard and Chet. Meanwhile, at ESPN we were all so new to network television that we just didn't know any better. We simply worked hard, endured any hardships, and tried to overcome the obstacles at hand. And, believe me, there were obstacles.

In 1981 we were doing a boxing show from the University of Illinois—Chicago Circle campus in a gym that would normally never have boxing inside it, so the ring had to be imported and constructed. We were about five minutes away from going on the air live when we noticed that the ring had not yet been completed. This was one of those thorny little details that somehow slipped through the cracks. Up in the ring was the local promoter Ernie Terrell, a former heavyweight champion, helping the crew finish putting the ring together. He started out in his business suit, but soon both jacket and tie were shed as desperation and perspiration increased.

When the clock struck 8pm and my broadcast partner, Sal Marchiano, and I were welcoming our viewers live at ringside, Ernie (now with shirttails hanging and sweat pouring), and his intrepid band of men were working feverishly on the ring in the background. Sal and I were done with the content we had planned and the producer nervously told us to keep talking. About five minutes later we were still talking and had pretty much run out of pertinent boxing topics. And still the ring was incomplete. Our stage manager yelled to Ernie, "The producer says we are starting the show NOW, no matter what. So get your men out of the ring." Ernie looked perplexed and worried, which pretty much describes Ernie's normal state, but this time it was *real* worry. To be sure, no one seemed certain that the ring was secure and ready for two hours of big men bouncing around in it. We trudged forward anyway, and throughout the show we all hoped no boxer would fall down through the middle of the ring. This might have been a first in boxing, a fatality caused not by the innate violence of the sport, but by faulty construction. We dodged this bullet as we would so many others on that series over the years.

Did I say bullet? On one 1980 *Top Rank Boxing* show in Chicago the crew very nearly had to dodge some real ones. The city of Chicago was not wired for cable in 1980 and so most Chicagoans certainly did not know anything about ESPN. An observant police officer saw a big truck with an ESPN logo on it parked outside the Aragon ballroom on the northwest side of the city. To him the letters ESPN were just as likely to have been Dan Quayle's misguided attempt at spelling the acronym for extrasensory perception as it would be a television network. So, when he saw someone going into the truck with a piece of audio equipment, he deduced that a robbery was in progress. Five minutes later the truck was surrounded by squad cars, and a few minutes after that police officers entered the truck, guns drawn and ready for business. A shaken producer eventually convinced them we were televising a boxing match and got them to stand down. Actually, the only crime committed that night came later when one of the boxers was robbed by the ringside judges of a well-earned decision.

Now that the letters ESPN are familiar to every male in the western hemisphere and many in the eastern one as well, this story reads like an episode out of the *Twilight Zone*. This story could have been set on some alternative universe. As delightful as it would be to think that we have a parallel universe that has not yet been sullied by Stephen A. Smith's commentaries or the *Around the Horn* show, I assure you this all took place right here on planet Earth.

In a postscript to this incident, there was still one obstacle to getting the show on the air that night. The police said that there was a "special permit" required for the truck to remain there—a permit that required several days to obtain. The ESPN operations manager said he had not been informed of such a permit and seemed amazed and horrified at all of this. I may have been new to network sportscasting, but as a lifelong resident of Chicago I was not new to how things worked back then. I told the operations manager that it seemed to me that the police were strongly suggesting that there might be some "alternative" way of handling this situation. It turned out I was correct: an agreement was reached, the truck stayed, and the show went on as planned. To this day I am not quite sure how that operations person listed that expenditure on his ESPN expense report.

A microcosm of all these early issues came during a show in Miami in 1982: the truck ESPN rented for the show blew a tire when it tried to park; most of the tape machines inside the truck were defective; the power cables were not long enough to reach the arena; and finally, no phone lines were installed. To solve the last problem they "appropriated" phone lines from a nearby construction site—which may not have been legal. But, the punishment for that was nothing compared to not getting on the air. It was twenty minutes before this show was to start when a technician made a harmless joke to the tense producer, who shot back, "Hey, this is no time for humor." That producer's statement in the truck years ago demonstrated one of many things he would be wrong about in his career. In thirty years around sports and television I have found that, intentional or not, there is always time for humor.

Beware of Anyone
Who Calls You Mister

Do you remember Ernest T. Bass on the Andy Griffith show? Ernest was a hermit who lived out in the woods and would occasionally make a foray into Mayberry to create havoc. His behavior was, shall we say, eccentric. For some reason, windows were his big enemy—he threw rocks at just about every one he saw. In each episode Ernest T. appeared in, Andy would labor while explaining his wild antics. Then Barney Fife would just shake his head, look at Andy, and say, "Ange, he's a nut."

And, so it is with Mike Tyson. After more than two decades of trying to explain his chaotic behavior, we are left with Barney's simple explanation—he's a nut.

I average about ten guest appearances per month on sports talk radio shows. That means that over the last thirty years I have done about three thousand of these shows, and on close to 90 percent of these appearances, at some point I have been asked to explain some aspect of Mike Tyson's behavior. Since I can barely explain *my* behavior in life, explaining Tyson's is a daunting task.

For about three years I explained his antisocial behavior by citing his hardships as a youth and his rejection by society. Then I had close to a four-year period of relying on the "betrayed by trusted friends and confidants" approach to give us the reason for his misdeeds. And, for a few years I really played "shrink" and theorized about some sort of chemical imbalance being at the root of his problems.

Finally, I settled on the Ernest T. Bass theory. The eloquent simplicity of this approach on radio shows had two advantages: First, it got the radio interviewers to laugh and move on so that we could get to the really important business at hand—plugging my upcoming pay-per-view telecast, live stage appearance, or record album. Second, it made it painfully obvious to the host that I was *only* qualified to comment on Tyson's left hook, defense, or razor quick incisors, capable of taking off an earlobe quicker than Hannibal Lecter. I was just a bit undertrained to psychoanalyze him.

My perspective on the Tyson phenomenon is somewhat unique in that I announced Tyson fights at the very beginning of his career and then at the end. In between I covered him for ESPN's *Sportscenter* from a slight distance, but not a long enough distance to prevent some intriguing and even contentious interviews.

Tyson's early matches were televised on ESPN's *Top Rank Boxing* series. He was a raw and powerful young fighter. I'd like to say that from the moment I saw him I recognized that he was destined to become a heavyweight icon. I'd like to say that, but a check of the videotapes of those broadcasts would prove me a bigger liar than Bernie Madoff.

There is one cardinal rule in evaluating a young heavyweight prospect that is knocking everybody out. That is that you *can't* evaluate him—at least not until he has faced someone who will:

A. punch back in earnest
B. take a good punch without falling down
C. both of the above.

In the half dozen or so Tyson fights I announced on ESPN, he never really faced anyone that fit those descriptions. So, the closest I came to anointing him a future king was this comment: "Mike Tyson has demonstrated the kind of quickness, power, and finishing ability that could carry him a long way." In retrospect that does make me look like a sage, until you realize that I said almost the exact same thing about Samson Po'uha and James Broad.

What *was* remarkable about Tyson at that time was his demeanor, which was nothing like the snarling and profane Tyson who later emerged. In the early 1980s he was unfailingly polite and cooperative. I remember sitting alone in a New York café during that time, and, coincidentally, Tyson was at another table with his manager Jimmy Jacobs. I went over to the table and said hello, to which Tyson replied, "Hi, Mr. Bernstein, nice to see you here." He then launched into a rhapsodic description of some Joe Louis fights he had been watching from the extensive fight film collection that Jacobs owned. He extolled Joe's virtues both inside and outside the ring and said one day he would like to be a champion just like him.

Was that Mike Tyson simply a creation of his own Machiavellian mind, constructed to "put one over" on the people covering him in the media? Was it all just a well-rehearsed act, orchestrated by his management team to maximize what was already amazingly positive news coverage? Or was Tyson at that time just a wide-eyed young man who was mesmerized by boxing history and thrilled that he was headed for that kind of center stage himself? The answer might be yes to all three of those questions—they could all have been operating simultaneously.

Now, flash forward about ten years to 1995 to a twenty-nine-year-old Tyson who takes the stage at the MGM Grand in Las Vegas for weigh-in for his match with Peter McNeeley. After three years in prison, Tyson was now back in the sport, and the weigh-in scene was something to behold. Several thousand fans were on hand, along with hundreds of media members, and the proceedings were being televised live to millions on ESPN.

One of the intriguing aspects of the lead-in to this match was, in fact, the kind of press on hand to cover the event. The dynamics were interesting because many women's groups were outraged that Tyson was again making millions as an athlete after his conviction and prison sentence on rape charges. It was, they felt, as if nothing had happened in the interim. This was especially galling to them because it seemed that part of the appeal of seeing Tyson back in the ring was a sense that somehow *he* had been victimized in this situation.

There was a pretty eclectic group of journalists reporting on this event. On the one hand we had the usual ink-stained wretches that cover boxing for the newspapers, a crusty and colorful group of testosterone-filled gents. On the other hand there were reporters (many of them women) from news organizations, women's magazines, and networks such as Lifetime. These were not the usual media outlets you see covering a boxing match. This was like an interfaith wedding—without the music and dancing.

A friend of mine who covered hard news for a national magazine was covering this fight for its news value. She surveyed the boxing media gathered at one of the press conferences for the fight and dryly asked me, "So, do you ever actually dine with any of these people?" I assured her that, for the most part, they all used knives and forks. I'm not sure she believed me. The irony was that all the additional coverage actually benefited the event. So, while many women's advocacy groups were fuming, the promoter of the fight, Don King, was secretly smiling over the furor.

In this group at the weigh-in were many reporters who had never covered a boxing weigh-in—and would likely never cover one again. One newscaster from an East Coast station came up to me and asked if I would do a brief guest shot with her for her early evening newscast. Off camera she asked me if weigh-ins were always like this. I told her that no, this was not the norm, that this is to weigh-ins what the Super Bowl is to football. When this analogy produced only a blank stare from her, I realized that she was not a sports fan, so my allegedly clever analogy meant nothing. This mirrored my answer to her next question, "What does the boxer's weight mean in this fight?" To which I replied, "For these guys, virtually nothing." And that was the case because no conventional boxing factors mattered. Peter McNeeley probably couldn't beat Mike Tyson if he had a machete . . . and a handgun.

Then we did our on-camera interview where I was able to use my Ernest T. Bass analogy for about the one-thousandth time, and she laughed. OK, I know what you're thinking, "Can't this guy ever have an original thought?" Well, I will refer you to Rodney Dangerfield who once said to me, "Al, I have two important pieces of advice for you." He said in a soft, almost reverent tone, "First, if it works, never stop using it." He paused for a moment, so I asked him, "What's second?" He leaned closer to me and screamed in my ear, "IF IT WORKS, NEVER STOP USING IT!" Damaged eardrum and all, I have lived by that credo.

After the interview, this newscaster asked me off camera if there were any aspect of this whole situation that seemed bizarre to me. I sighed, shook my head, and said, "Everything."

This weigh-in was a tense situation because Tyson and his camp were very unhappy with ESPN's coverage of his rape trial, his stay in prison, and his pending return to the sport. Charley Steiner from *Sportscenter* did most of that coverage—I did not have a lead role in all that. I was, however, most certainly the face of boxing on ESPN at that time. So a portion of the Team Tyson venom was directed at me.

After a series of negotiations that rivaled the Paris peace talks, ESPN got the Tyson people to agree to have him do a very brief interview on the live telecast right after he stepped down from the scales at the weigh-in. In front of this large live throng and millions watching on ESPN, Tyson mounted the scales and weighed in at 220 pounds. I chronicled that and started a preamble to our interview. As I continued to talk, I noticed that Tyson sat down on a chair (not what we had planned) and he very slowly started putting on his T-shirt, and then, even more slowly, lacing his shoes. All the while I was vamping to beat the band. And here I should explain that on live television, when you are filling time, seconds can seem like minutes and minutes an eternity. And that is precisely what I was doing. I had a strange sensation when I thought I saw a little smile curl up on Tyson's lips as he quickly glanced at me. Wow, I thought, he's enjoying this. At that moment it didn't take an investigative reporter to figure out that he was doing this on purpose. Finally, after I had run out of pertinent information and was considering a discussion of foreign policy, I decided to lean down to where he was sitting and still slowly tying knots on his shoes, and I said, "Well, now let's see if we can hear from former heavyweight champion Mike Tyson." I leaned closer and said, "Mike, can we talk to you now?" He looked up at me, flashed a devilish smile and said, "No f$@#ing way." I paused briefly to drink this moment in, turned to the camera and said, "I'll take that as a no, back to you Charley."

Apparently we had come a long way from "Hi, Mr. Bernstein, nice to see you."

Unlike Reality TV,
Live Sports Television Is Actually Real

In the wonderful movie *My Favorite Year*, set in the 1950s, aging movie star Alan Swann (played expertly by Peter O'Toole) is just about ready for his guest appearance on the *King Kaiser* show, and he says, "I feel so good I think I'll get it in one take." A young producer responds with a chuckle, "Here we always get it in one take—it's live." A horrified Swann asks, "Live, what do you mean live? You mean everything we say just spills out there for people to hear?". The producer says, "Well . . . yes." Alan replies, "I can't do that. I'm not an actor. I'm a movie star."

In live sports television it all just "spills out" to everyone as it happens. And so it is exhilarating to do live sports television—but there is no delete button. In thirty years of doing this I have seen, and been responsible for, some noteworthy gaffes. Except for the only perfect sportscaster, Bob Costas, we have all had our moments. Well, come to think of it, even Bob may have made a mistake once in the 1990s . . . or was it the 80s?

If sportscasters have had their share of imprudent or mistaken comments, active participants in sporting events have had even more. These things happen either because someone is nervous about being on television or they are so relaxed they forget they are on television. Except for comedians on cable networks who do it on purpose, most people curse on TV because it is part of their DNA and they forget they are live to the world.

One such person was a lightweight boxer named Kenny "Bang Bang" Bogner, who was a frequent combatant on the ESPN *Top Rank Boxing* series in the early 1980s. He was always in exciting fights—his 1982 win over Kato Wilson was judged the best ESPN fight of that year. He had a large and vocal fan base in the Atlantic City, New Jersey, area, and they were there in force for his fight with Wilson. I was trying to interview him in the ring after the win, and his adoring fans were still cheering wildly. I asked him a question about how he achieved his victory and he squinted at me as though he could not hear, so I repeated the question. He responded, "Al, I didn't hear a f$@#ing word you said." So, I leaned in closer and asked the question as loud as I could. He responded, "Oh! Now I hear you. I didn't hear a f$@#ing word you said before." After that, his answer to the question was a bit anticlimactic.

As a side note to this, a year later Kenny was scheduled to fight Ray Mancini for the world lightweight title, but a Mancini shoulder injury derailed the match. For that fight Frank Sinatra was actually scheduled to be a commentator at ringside and do interviews on the telecast. I've always wondered—if Old Blue Eyes would have been faced with a similar situation with Bogner inside the ring. I'm sure Frank would have been deeply offended, having never heard that kind of language before.

Ever since microphones found their way into boxing corners in the 1980s, we have been treated to some colorful and entertaining monologues from trainers. I remember one who spent about fifty seconds of the one-minute break berating his fighter with a profanity-laced diatribe that would make Sarah Silverman blush. Then he looked at the cameraman, got a horrified look on his face and shouted "Oh f$@#, I'm on TV."

Many have been mistaken about the round number as they dispensed advice to a fighter. On an ESPN show in the early 1990s, a trainer told his fighter that it was the last round coming up. The boxer looked at him and said, "No it's not." Trying to save face, the trainer said, "Oh, right, I was testing you." Gee, the previous thirty minutes of him getting punched wasn't the real test?

Another time a trainer got into the ring and started his instructions when a particularly exquisite ring-card girl went by their corner. As if it were choreographed, both the trainer and fighter swiveled their heads to follow her progress. The trainer interrupted his instructions with one word, "Jeez." Then he went back to talking boxing. When the scene ended, my witty broadcast partner Barry Tompkins wryly commented, "See, it takes concentration to be a great athlete." So, there was an example of perfectly chosen words delivered well by a sportscaster. Oh, if it were only always so.

After Sal Marchiano left ESPN in 1982, there was a six-year period before Barry Tompkins arrived for his almost eight-year stint as my partner. During that six-year interim period just about everyone who ever passed through ESPN headquarters in Bristol, Connecticut, appeared at least once as my broadcast partner. During one stretch of our weekly boxing series I worked with eight different partners in eight weeks. One fellow, whose name mercifully I really can't remember so he can be anonymous, was as nervous as anyone I have ever worked with. He had a deer-in-the-headlights look on his face for two-and-a-half hours and hung on by his fingernails until the final moments of the telecast, and then he lost his grip. He closed the show by saying, "So I'm Al Bernstein for my partner (his name), saying goodnight." Ouch.

Wit was not restricted to Barry on the ESPN *Top Rank Boxing* series. Sal demonstrated it while covering up for a rookie mistake I made in 1981. We were in an empty arena in Worcester, Massachusetts, doing the close of a show. Normally, when we went to video highlights of the show on screen, we were never put back on camera again. So, while Sal was wrapping things up with the highlights showing, I took off my microphone, got up, and started to leave. At that precise moment they came back to us on camera, just in time to see me exiting the shot. Sal said, "We will see you next week in Atlantic City, and that's Al getting a head start." I never did that again, but I have done other things.

As of the writing of this book I am still gainfully employed as the boxing analyst on *Showtime Championship Boxing*—by far the best job I have ever had on television. The fact that I still have that job is an indication that the folks who run Showtime have a sense of humor. I'll explain. We were doing a match in 2009 from the Home Depot Center, just outside of Los Angeles. I was on camera with Steve Albert, and I was supposed to make a comment about the fans who had braved rain showers to come out to the event. When it was my turn to talk I said,

"And these great fans have braved the elements to see boxing tonight at the Home Box Office Center." Home Box Office, of course, stands for HBO, Showtime's competitor. At that moment the sound I imagined hearing was the gnashing of teeth by Showtime executives across the country in New York. Steve rescued the moment by saying, "Well, Al, I guess you just had your YouTube moment." Indeed I had.

Some sixteen years earlier I barely escaped what surely could have been an embarrassing episode. I was assigned to do a pay-per-view fight and arrived in Phoenix two days before the card. Then I contracted perhaps the worst stomach flu I have ever had. For about forty-eight hours I stayed in my hotel room and threw up. It was beyond horrible. On the day of the fight I was barely able to get dressed and go to the arena. My broadcast partner for the evening was the very gifted Sam Rosen. He took one look at me and said, "You need help." That was an understatement. Someone found the ring doctor and brought him over. I explained what was going on and he said, "No problem, I'll fix you up." He gave me a shot for the nausea and I was feeling better in a remarkably short period of time.

What that doctor forgot to mention is that those shots can also make you very drowsy. About thirty minutes into the telecast my eyelids were drooping. Every time my head slumped forward a bit, Sam elbowed me in the side to wake me up. I contributed precious little of note to that telecast—Sam carried me through the whole thing, and I know there were a few rounds where I nodded off to sleep briefly. The intriguing part of all of this is that no one commented on my lack of contributions, which either spoke to Sam's excellence or the low expectations people had of me. I'm rooting for the former, not the latter. We can all name television personalities who have put viewers to sleep with their commentary—but I may be the only one who ever succeeded in putting *himself* to sleep during a broadcast. That takes true talent.

I admire and respect Marvin Hagler as much as any athlete in history. He's a great boxer and a stand-up guy. He and I have always had an excellent relationship. So, it is ironic that my two worst on-the-air mistakes were saved for Marvin's fights. Both mistakes slightly tarnished important moments in his career.

The first came in 1985 after his win over Tommy Hearns. I

announced the fight with Al Michaels on pay-per-view, and after Hagler's stirring KO win in round 3, I said the following: "This amazing victory more than compensates for his loss to Roberto Duran." Well, as any casual boxing fan knows, Marvin did *not* lose to Duran, something I certainly knew, since I also announced that fight on pay-per-view.

Hagler won a close decision over Duran in which many felt he was too passive against the smaller Hands of Stone. He won nonetheless, and probably by a wider margin than the judges' scorecards indicated. I wanted to say in my comment after the Hearns win that Hagler had surely put to rest any criticism he may have gotten for not stopping Duran. What came out of my mouth was unfortunately *not* that thought.

We now flash forward to 1986 and the fight between Hagler and John Mugabi. Hagler had scored an exciting TKO win in the 11th round, and I was up in the ring interviewing him about the win. We were nearing the end of the interview and the producer said something in my ear that went a little longer than it should have, and I did not hear all of one of Marvin's statements. The part I heard was: "Would you all mind if I left?" I thought he meant he wanted to end the interview, so I said, "No problem Marvin, you worked hard enough tonight, congratulations." Then I turned back to the camera to do a final analysis of the evening, as planned, leaving a slightly befuddled Marvin Hagler in my wake. As the great Paul Harvey used to say, here is the rest of the story.

The full comment that Marvin had made in the interview was, "Since this is my 12th title defense, maybe it's time to retire, would you all mind if I left?" Well, by missing the first part of that statement, and dismissing Marvin, I was ignoring a potential retirement announcement on the air from boxing's biggest name. So . . . that went well. Only later did I find out about my blunder—I did not sleep very much that night.

These two incidents make it look like I was dedicated to trying to ruin Marvin Hagler's legacy. However, in between these two incidents I gave him hundreds of richly deserved compliments on the air. So, apparently I was actually more intent on ruining *my* career. Somehow I survived those two mistakes made on boxing's center stage.

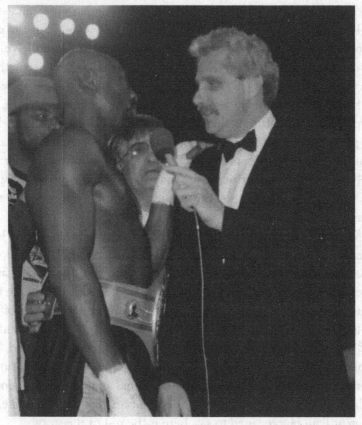

This was a familiar scene in the 1980's. I interviewed Marvelous Marvin Hagler after yet another of his title wins in a big pay-per-view match. In one of these post fight interviews with Marvin I committed a bit of a faux pas. OK, that's the polite way of saying I screwed up.

Sometimes on live television, craziness is thrust upon you through no fault of your own. We often did our ESPN *Top Rank Boxing* shows from various spots in Massachusetts. A good number of the fans there were, well, let's say enthusiastic. Ok, maybe I can go so far as to say they were a little out of control. Wait, what's the word I'm searching for . . . oh, yes . . . NUTS! Alcohol was usually involved in their erratic behavior. Some of it was a bit hostile, like the time in Brockton when Sal Marchiano and I were doing our on-camera open to the show, and for reasons known only to them, the fans right in front of us started to chant, "You guys suck." I was only about one-and-a-half years into my sportscasting career, and I don't mind telling you I was a bit rattled. I fought my way through the comments I was supposed to make, looking at these angry and raucous souls out of the corner of my eye—to make sure they weren't rushing us. Sal, on the other hand, was chuckling and said on the air, "I guess you can hear how much they love us here in Brockton, we'll be back with our first bout right away, so stay with us." As we sat down at ringside during the commercial I said to Sal. 'Wow, this is crazy." He said, "Hey, it could be worse, at least nobody's throwing anything. Wait until that happens."

Well, I knew that from time to time fans at a boxing match would get a bit disturbed at a decision or a fight stoppage and toss a few items toward the ring—you know, coins, bottles, spouses . . . whatever they could lay their hands on. But, what I did not realize, and most people don't think about, is that a television commentator is the most vulnerable person in that arena under those circumstances. Why? *Because we can't move.* We are tied to our spot by the cords of the headsets and the fact that we are on live television, so we can't leave.

Over these thirty some years I have been ringside when crowds have been a bit distressed and chose to vent their anger by throwing things at the ring. Amazingly, for almost twenty-nine of those years, I avoided any genuine direct hits—oh, once or twice something grazed off my back, but nothing worrisome. Then came San Juan, Puerto Rico, in 2011. Hometown hero Juan Manuel Lopez was defending his featherweight title against Mexico's Orlando Salido. Lopez was undefeated and the favorite in the fight. But, apparently no one told Salido this, and he spent the first seven rounds blasting Lopez around the ring—even putting him down once. In the 8th round Salido landed a couple of good punches and stunned Lopez, but Lopez had actually been hurt worse earlier in the fight, and he is famous for his resiliency. And, the referee was from Puerto Rico. So, you wouldn't expect a quick stoppage there. You wouldn't expect it, but that's exactly what happened.

Even though Lopez may well have been stopped in the next minute or next round or later, this was odd timing for the stoppage. The fans were somewhat justifiably upset. So naturally, they started pelting the ring with objects. I was a bit oblivious to the items raining down at first, because I was concentrating on doing the replays. Ironically I was in midsentence suggesting that the booing fans may have a point about the stoppage being a bit too soon, when a full water bottle hit me about a quarter-inch from my right eye. It hit so hard the thud could be clearly heard on the air through my microphone. I gave an audible groan from shock and pain. Gus Johnson, my broadcast partner for the evening, announced, "My partner has been hit."

One of Gus' charms as a sportscaster is his ability to capture the drama of the moment, and perhaps enhance it a bit—well, one might surmise from his call that a sniper had shot me. But, however heated, his description was accurate—and I had a cut and a bruise under my right eye to prove it. I took my headset off to get myself together—I was dazed to be sure. A minute later I was talking on the broadcast again, but with an aching face and a headache to beat the band. It dawned on me later that I could have said something really loopy on the air—I was still a bit groggy. But, then, given some of the on-air gaffes I have admitted to in this chapter, how much worse could I have done, and in this case I would have had a built-in excuse.

It's actually a miracle that it took twenty-nine years of broadcasting fights to get hit on the head with something. It's as if all the people throwing things all those years had the kind of aim it takes to be a Chicago Cubs pitcher. I received e-mails, tweets, and letters from many Puerto Rican fans who apologized for their countrymen—which was very nice but completely unnecessary. The Puerto Rican boxing fans are among the nicest and most knowledgeable in the world. Besides, I'm sure that bottle wasn't meant for me . . . unless of course, Marvin Hagler was there that night and he was just getting even.

Father Knows Best

OK, this undeniable truth may have come exceptions like Joe Jackson, John Phillips, Marv Marinovich, and any dad who ever let his child sleep overnight at the Neverland Ranch. Yes, there are plenty of fathers that may not know best, but let's not quibble. How about we just agree that the dads I will talk about in this chapter knew best, and perhaps we can say that on some level the vast majority of fathers have some wisdom to offer to their children. Here's a good example.

On a summer night in 1960 the Chicago Cubs had mounted a rally in the 8th inning against the Cincinnati Reds. They did it at the expense of a young relief pitcher just called up from the minors. After the Reds' manager removed him from the game, this pitcher was the picture of dejection as he trudged back to the dugout.

Watching this scene unfold on television was a ten-year-old Cubs fan. He was so elated that he felt the need, there in his living room, to taunt the dejected pitcher. He got up and pointed at the screen and said, "Yeah, you got nothin' kid, back to the minors for you." A moment later the screen went black. The young boy looked befuddled that this rare moment of Cubs-induced joy had suddenly disappeared.

His father, normally a gentle and some might say too lenient parent, had shut the television off. In a stern voice he told his son, "Just because your team is doing well doesn't mean you have to attack that pitcher personally. You never do that to an athlete or anyone else for failing.

Would you want someone doing that to you? If you ever do that again you will never watch baseball with me in this house."

Because his dad had *never* talked to him that way before, the ten-year-old got the message and immediately felt ashamed for his outburst. He said only, "I'm sorry, Dad." The game resumed and the boy never spoke that way about an athlete again. The boy and his father watched in harmony as many sporting events as they could after that, but the number was far too few because the father died of cancer less than two years later.

The father's name was Sol Bernstein, and I have never forgotten the lesson my dad taught me on that summer night. Without knowing it at the time, he gave me the cornerstone of my approach to sports writing and broadcasting. I have tried very hard as a commentator to live up to the standard my father set for me that night.

If my dad were still alive I am sure he would join me in my disgust for the recent trend in covering sports that allows and even encourages the most vile and personal criticism of sports figures. Even as a ten-year-old I got the point. You can accurately cover both the successes and failures of athletes, teams, or other sports figures, offering celebration of the former and responsible criticism of the latter without making your comments personal and degrading. When you offer only snide and degrading commentary you only degrade yourself. There will be more on that in chapter 8, but please don't skip ahead because you'll hate yourself for missing the next few chapters. In those I reveal the answers to three burning questions: 1.) Who really shot JFK? 2.) Where is the Loch Ness Monster? and 3.) How does Mel Kiper get his hair to look that way?

Meanwhile, back to this undeniable truth. In addition to baseball I watched boxing with my father. Well, first I listened to boxing "near" my father. When I was nine years old I would get out of bed and sneak down the stairs and sit just out of eyeshot of my dad and I would listen to the *Gillette Friday Night Fights* on television. I heard the voice of the great Don Dunphy calling the action. As I sat in the dark on that stairway listening and imagining how my dad was enjoying watching those fights, I hungered for two things. The first was to be old enough to go down and watch the boxing with my father, and the second was to some day grow up and be a sportscaster just like Don Dunphy.

Some months into this Friday night ritual I heard my mother come into the living room when my dad was watching the fights. I could barely make out their conversation. I did pick up the end of it, where my mother said with a grudging laugh, "OK, let him come down." Then my father called out to me, "Buddy boy (his pet name for me) come on down. You can watch the fights." He obviously knew all along that I was lurking on the stairway, and on this night his lobbying efforts with my mother had finally paid off. I bolted down the stairs and took up a position on the floor near my father's easy chair. With supreme joy I watched my first boxing match on television. This became a Friday night ritual that I will always treasure.

Those Friday night fights featured greats like Emile Griffith, Dick Tiger, Carmen Basilio, Gene Fullmer, and Archie Moore. Those fighters were wonderful, but there was one boxer who completely stole my heart. With the exception of my Chicago Cubs hero Ernie Banks, no athlete then or since has captivated me more than Sugar Ray Robinson. He is regarded as the greatest boxer who ever lived, and equally important he had a panache and style that was impossible to resist. He didn't have to call attention to himself. Simply by being Sugar Ray he demanded that you pay attention to him. How could you not? He would enter the ring as the embodiment of elegant simplicity. Wearing a tasteful black or white robe tied in the front, his hair slicked back to accentuate his movie star looks, he would move in his corner with an ease and elegance that let you know you were about to see something special.

By the time I got to see him he was already thirty-nine years old, certainly not in his prime. Amazingly he was still one of the best middleweights in the world, and he made the night of December 3, 1960, one I will never forget. Sugar Ray fought Gene Fullmer to try and reclaim the middleweight title. Gene was twenty-nine years old and defending the crown for the fourth time. Sugar Ray had knocked him out with a thunderous left hook the previous time they met in the ring, but that was three years earlier. Sugar Ray was the decided underdog for this match.

These two men were as different as two people could be. Sugar Ray was a dazzling urbanite from New York City who lived the high life. He appeared as a tap dancer on national television variety shows and was one of the first boxers to really cross over as a show biz celeb. Fullmer, on the other hand, was a Mormon from West Jordan, Utah. He was the very definition of a blue-collar type of guy who worked as a welder before turning to pro boxing.

Inside the ring they were also a stark contrast to each other. Even at thirty-nine Robinson was poetry in motion, a textbook boxer-puncher who did just about everything right. His movement was fluid, as if he had choreographed the fight like one of his dance routines. And with the beautiful movement came picture-perfect combination punching. Fullmer was a plodding fighter who would bludgeon foes into submission. He was all about the will to win. Make no mistake, he knew how to fight, but compared to Robinson he looked like an unskilled laborer. In his defense, almost everyone looked like that when compared to Sugar Ray. What Gene Fullmer did know how to do was win, and he did so fifty-five times in his career.

On that December night in 1960 Sugar Ray Robinson defeated Father Time. Over fifteen grueling rounds he boxed beautifully against the younger Fullmer. He summoned up something special inside that thirty-nine-year-old body that had been through 150 fights in a twenty-year career. He out boxed Gene and out punched him too, landing more punches and the harder shots. Yes, he beat Father Time, but he did not beat the judges. Somehow this match was officially ruled a draw, allowing Fullmer to keep his world title. The referee, who scored back then, made the fight 11 rounds to 4 for Robinson, while one judge inexplicably gave Fullmer 9 rounds and scored him the winner. The final judge ruled it a draw 7–7–1. When the decision was announced I nearly pierced my father's eardrums by screaming "No, they can't do that!" Nearly all of the writers at ringside thought Sugar Ray had won the match, and the crowd reaction told us that they thought so too.

As a fan and broadcaster I have gnashed my teeth many times since over what appeared to be terrible decisions, but none ever had the impact that that one did on me as a ten-year-old boy. Perhaps this was good training for being a lifelong Cubs fan where disappointment and frustration is simply a way of life. At the time, however, I was devastated. I cried myself to sleep.

Like most sports fans that have seen their favorite team or athlete lose, I let my irrational side take over. I wasn't just mad at the judges for their act of larceny—I saw Gene Fullmer as the villain as well. How, I wondered, could he even accept such a tainted draw—and have the nerve to say in the postfight interview that he thought he won? How could he even wear that championship belt with any pride? I was a ten-year-old scorned, and Gene was one of the targets of my ire. My preteen and then teenage mind directed me to root against Gene whenever he fought. That would teach him.

As I got older I realized that Gene Fullmer was as far from being a villain as anyone could ever be. In fact, Gene is a wonderful guy. When I first met him at the 75th Anniversary Gala of *Ring Magazine*, he was humorous and delightful and very complimentary of my announcing. That gave me a great feeling, and made me feel a bit guilty for rooting against him as a youngster. I see Gene and his family every year at the International Hall of Fame inductions. Ironically, his wife Karen is a Chicago native who also lives the hard life of a Cubs fan. She is quite simply one of the most charming people you could ever meet.

Of course, the man who announced that Robinson-Fullmer fight on television and all the rest of the *Friday Night Fight* series was the great Don Dunphy. While I had tremendous admiration for Sugar Ray Robinson, I was nearly as awestruck by Don. When I first saw Don on television he was at the height of an amazing career. He had been a versatile all-around radio sportscaster in the 1930s, with great knowledge of baseball and track and field. He had been a distance runner at Manhattan College. Then in 1941 he started doing the *Friday Night Fight* series on radio and became the voice of boxing. So, Don was my chosen role model and I would find out later in life that I chose wisely.

In 1985 The ESPN *Top Rank Boxing* series was moving to Friday night, and as a part of that someone came up with the very good idea to have me interview the official voice of those *Gillette Friday Night Fights* . . . the very same Don Dunphy. So I was to share the television stage with the man who fueled my desire to become a sportscaster. Along with my excitement to meet him I had some concerns. What if I did not do a really good interview with him? Did he even like my work as a broadcaster? Finally, what if, as so often is the case, up close and personal my hero turned out to not be as genial and supportive as I imagined he would be? I felt like how the character of Rachel Berry on *Glee* would feel if she were going to meet Barbra Streisand.

During preproduction for one of our Atlantic City ESPN *Top Rank Boxing* shows, Don showed up for the interview. He strode right up to me with the same smile I had seen so often on television and said, "Gee, Al, it's so good to meet you." Vintage Don Dunphy—a simple statement uncluttered by extra verbiage. It was his warm smile and affectionate handshake that made me feel he really meant what he said. Minus the romance it was the same feeling I would later have in meeting my wife Connie—I melted.

We taped a seven-minute interview (huge in length for an element put into coverage of a live sports event), and it went very well. He offered insights and shared anecdotes that reminded me of why I admired him so much. Then he told me how much he enjoyed the interview and we exchanged phone numbers. From that moment on he became a friend and a mentor. We would talk on the phone and discuss boxing and broadcasting.

I started as an analyst, but by the mid 1980s I was also hosting (play-by-play) boxing shows. In developing a method and style of doing play-by-play, I consciously took elements from the work of Don and two of my ESPN partners, Sal Marchiano and Sam Rosen. Later I would be influenced by working with Barry Tompkins, Bob Papa, and Steve Albert. Hey, at least we can say this—I only steal from the best!

I don't mind saying that I was influenced by those talented men, listening closely to what they did as I worked beside them. You can endow your work with elements of what others do without doing an impression of them. You can certainly leave room for your own originality to shine through.

When Don Dunphy worked on television in the 1950s and 1960s, he almost always worked alone. He was not only a skilled host (as evidenced by his work in other sports), but also he knew boxing well enough to add some additional comments that offered viewers analysis of the fight as well. He felt strongly that boxing should be commentated by one person and one alone. God knows what he would think of the three-man announce teams that are so prevalent today.

In fact, for the first Muhammad Ali-Joe Frazier fight in 1971, Don would not share the microphone with a movie star. This event, Don believed, was too important to boxing history to become a mere show business spectacle. The promoters, who came from the theatrical world, had actually hired Burt Lancaster to do color commentating for the event. Don steadfastly told the promoters, "I am working these rounds solo. Mr. Lancaster can talk only between rounds." Wouldn't you know it, Mr. Lancaster got a little excited during one round and started to talk. Don simply put his hand over Burt's microphone to prevent that from happening. Mr. Dunphy had the last word on this.

I actually did announce fights on my own at ESPN. In 1986 some decision maker (possibly a descendant of the Marquis de Sade), decided it would be an interesting experiment to have me work a two-and-a-half-hour *Top Rank* show alone. It's probably hard for many of you to imagine that happening, but since I am not one of those "drink cocktails at the pool and tell exaggerated stories to a ghostwriter" kind of guy, I can assure you this really happened. It was tricky on many fronts—one being that I also had to interview the fighters after each fight, so it took some creativity to segue into and out of those.

I fought my way through it all. I must say, I was impressed with my analyst that night—a very insightful chap. Oh, wait, that was me too. Actually, I was just relieved to get through the night in one piece and get the job done. Don called me the next day and said, "See, that's the way to do boxing, you don't need anyone else with you. Tell them you want to do the shows alone. It was great." While I appreciated his praise more than anything I could possibly hear, I didn't have the heart to remind Don that when he did the Friday night fights alone, every show was one hour, and almost always one fight. The idea of doing a two-and-a-half-hour show with three to four fights forty-eight weeks out of the year seemed a little daunting, even to a thirty-six-year-old who *loved* sportscasting.

Don provided me with the two proudest moments of my career. The first came when Don was asked in a magazine article "Who is your favorite boxing announcer?" He replied simply, "Al Bernstein is my favorite—I really enjoy listening to him." I remember thinking at that moment, whatever happens the rest of my career, I now had all the validation I needed. To paraphrase Sally Fields at the Academy Awards, "HE LIKES ME!"

The other big moment came at the 75th Anniversary Celebration of *Ring Magazine*. It was a grand event and Don was to receive the award as the greatest boxing announcer of all time. He asked that I present the award to him. As I got ready to go on stage to present the award I wished more than anything that my father could be there to see this. Don had been a link to my father . . . to those treasured moments we spent watching boxing matches chronicled by the great Don Dunphy.

One of my proudest moments came when legendary broadcaster Don Dunphy asked that I present him with the Ring Magazine award as best boxing announcer of all time. This 75th Anniversary Gala of Ring was a magical night. Only having my father there would have made it better.

All this came full circle in 2003 when I joined Showtime Networks as a boxing analyst on the *Showtime Championship Boxing* series. The director of that series is Bob Dunphy, Don's son. Like his father, Bob is not only great at his job, but also the most gracious of men. Bob has been the director of the Showtime series since its inception in 1989. He has also had a seventeen-year, award-winning stint as a director for CBS sports where he did all the major sporting events, including major boxing matches. From 1941 to 2012 the Dunphy family has been a major force in bringing the sport of boxing to the public. That's more than remarkable.

Just as I started watching the fights with my father on television at age ten, Bob and his brother Don Jr. (who has also had a successful career in television in New York), started going to the fights in person with their dad. I was excited just to get to watch them on television—imagine how Bob felt accompanying his dad, the voice of boxing, to the Mecca of boxing, Madison Square Garden. All this during a golden age for the sport. Bob said, "I remember going to The Garden and my brother Don Jr. and I were sitting about ten rows back when the crowd started buzzing. We looked around and there was Sugar Ray Robinson, with a gorgeous woman on each arm. He walked down the aisle to his seat and waved to the crowd. They went crazy."

Bob, who played the outfield at Notre Dame, learned about baseball, boxing, and television from his dad. And he learned discipline that was enhanced by both his and his father's education at Catholic schools from grade school to college. Don was not an authoritarian as a parent—he was a soft-spoken and gentle man (much like my father). Still, he had a no-nonsense approach to getting the job done that was passed on to his sons.

Bob learned something from his dad's straightforward, no-frills approach to covering boxing matches. "When directing a live sports event you can mess it up by being too creative," Bob said. He added, "You have to make sure you present the event properly. You can't make a terrible fight better with creative directing, but you can ruin a good fight." The idea is simple—serve the viewer. That was Don Dunphy's credo.

While Don was not a negative announcer, he also refused to try and make a terrible fight better by selling it too hard. Bob remembers that at one point some executives at Madison Square Garden were upset with Don's call of a not-so-thrilling fight. He said, "The *New York Post* ran a story defending my father, and in that story my father said, 'I won't fake it if a fight is not good.' He did not back down."

Just as my father taught me a lesson in civility in my own living room that would help me as a sportscaster, Don taught lessons by example that his sons would put to good use in their television careers. His dad's work and his legacy is never lost on Bob. "I always travel with my father's credential from the George Foreman-Joe Frazier fight. I keep it in my briefcase and it goes with me to every boxing match I direct. It always will."

I have one child, a twelve-year-old named Wes. He did not get the memo that his dad is a sportscaster. His passion and talent is in acting and music. If you mention an Oscar to him, he does not think De La Hoya, he thinks Academy Award. I have no problem relating to his interest because I love theater and music as well. Even if didn't I would still be watching the show *Glee* with him every Tuesday night to share the experience. That's why dads were invented.

One of our yearly rituals is watching the Tony Awards together. To us and to millions of others it is a magical night when the best in theater show respect to each other, dazzle us with their talents, and often reveal something of their soul. In some ways don't boxers do the same? Wes and I revel in those Tony moments the same way my father and I did while watching those Friday night fights. Whether it's the cast of *Memphis* bringing the blues to life through song and dance, or a thirty-nine-year-old Sugar Ray Robinson finding the fountain of youth against Gene Fullmer, both are moments worth freezing in time. I look at Wes watching the Tony awards and I know he is dreaming of one day being on that show, just as I watched those fights and dreamed of being Don Dunphy.

Some of the most enjoyable moments for me a sportscaster are when a father and son approach me to say hello or take a photo. I hope that in some small measure I am a part of some special moments for them, just as Don Dunphy was for me and my dad.

Even in this sometimes jaded era of sports and sports broadcasting, I like to think sportscasters can help create lasting memories for a father and son watching on television. I know it's true when I get to visit with a dad and son like these two. (Photo by Pearsi Bastiany/Impact Photos)

UNDENIABLE TRUTH #5:

It's Possible
to Be a Successful Failure

On the list of people that are expected to be funny, boxers probably rank just behind German automobile engineers.

That is one big misconception. Boxers can be very funny, and the funniest of them all is Bruce "The Mouse" Strauss. The Mouse fought his entire thirteen-year career as an "opponent." That is a fighter who is slightly or more than slightly overmatched in most of his fights. He goes into other fighters' hometowns to test young prospects or fight contenders who need a tune-up fight. Wins don't come too often or too easily. For a career opponent—and Mouse is the best of all time—failure is likely at least 50 percent of the time, and depending on how you achieve that failure, well, you can be a success. In fact, he lists as one of his achievements that he was knocked out on every continent except Antarctica.

The Mouse lost with style, panache, and humor. He actually turned losing into an art form. His official record is listed at 77–53–6, but he probably had closer to two hundred fights. He estimates that he won about a hundred fights and lost about a hundred fights. When you think of it, there are a couple of NBA coaches in the Hall of Fame who just barely won more games than they lost—so this might work in other sports, but in boxing a .500 record is not something to brag about.

From his home base in Omaha, Nebraska, Mouse would travel a

couple hundred thousand miles per year by car to fight whenever and wherever a promoter would put him on the card. He often fought under assumed names, sometimes three nights a week. In fact he fought twice in one night. He got knocked out in a preliminary fight, and when one of the main event fighters did not show up he told the promoter, "Put me in there. I'll put different color trunks on, change my hair a little, and we'll say it's my twin." Fight he did and, you guessed it, he got knocked out again.

In 1980 he fought on an ESPN card in which contender Bobby Czyz knocked him out. The next night he showed up in Nebraska to fight. As he was walking to the ring a fan yelled out, "Hey, is that the bum I saw get knocked out last night on TV?" Mouse yelled back, "No that was The Moose. I'm The Mouse."

His philosophy was that he would punch as hard as he could in a fight, for as long as he could, and try to win, but when that was not possible, he would surrender. But, he would surrender in a dramatic fashion that made the hometown hero look especially good. He claims he never actually took a dive and in fact needed to try and win because it was part of his job description. "If I could beat a guy, then his manager and promoter should know about it, then they can stop putting money into him as a prospect."

And, while he denigrated his ability (he certainly was not a great boxer), he was a clever fighter who knew how to control the pace of a fight when confronted with an opponent that he could handle. He once did something I have never seen anyone else do in a boxing ring. In 1981 I was announcing a card for a regional channel in the Midwest. Mouse was fighting Jimmy Baker, who was then undefeated in six fights. For the entire six rounds Mouse fought off the ropes just above my announce position at ringside. He *never* allowed the match to be fought anywhere else, constantly luring Baker right back to that spot. He won a decision and afterward I asked him why he did that. He said, "Well, Al, to be honest I didn't want to miss any of your commentary. I could hear it from that spot. I really enjoyed it. You did a good job tonight." Amazing.

He never trained; he just fought. He actually thought training would ruin his career as an opponent. "Look," he said, "If I trained I would be in better shape to go longer and sustain more punishment, I wouldn't be able to fight as much." It's hard to challenge that logic.

In the age before there was a computerized system of tracking fighters, he fought under dozens of phony names. Sometimes he would actually use the name of someone he didn't like, lose the fight, and then mail that person the newspaper clipping of the loss. Once he outsmarted himself. He showed up at a venue fighting under his real name. His opponent never showed up at the weigh-in, and no one could find him. Finally Mouse realized that his opponent was an alias *he* had previously fought under. Somehow he had also been booked under the phony name to fight that night—he was matched against *himself*!

At the core of all this is the fact that Mouse was always a charming guy. No one could be easier or more delightful to interact with. He cared about his fellow "opponents," with whom he often traveled on the road to fights. A group of the Midwestern fighters who did this were even named The Mousketeers. And on the road let no one mess with his comrades and friends. He may have frequently lost in the ring, but he seldom lost outside it. He was a hellacious street fighter when the occasion called for it, yet another of the fascinating contradictions in his life.

The computerized tracking of fighters and the many punches he absorbed contributed to the end of his career. His last official fight was in 1989. He simply couldn't do what he had done for more than a decade—the jig was up. There was a delightful movie, "The Mouse," made about his nomadic story in the mid 1990s. It was a good movie, but it did not make much money at the box office. Like Bruce's career, it was a successful failure.

ESPN Used to Stand
for Sports Programming Network
with No Mustaches

It's a semi-obscure fact that the ESPN acronym stands for Entertainment and Sports Programming Network. Bill Rasmussen, the eccentric founder of ESPN, named it that because he envisioned his creation featuring an entertainment lineup as well as sports.

How then, you may ask, could it be an undeniable truth that ESPN really stood for sports programming with no mustaches? That question deserves an answer and if I didn't have one I would be losing one of my "truths"—something I can ill afford this early in the book. In the 1980s and 1990s, ESPN executives viewed mustaches the way the Tea Party views taxes. In fact, Rand Paul would be green with envy at how effective ESPN management was in cutting mustaches in those two decades. They had a surplus of clean-shaven upper lips.

At least half dozen ESPN personalities, including the likes of Chris Berman and Chris Mortensen, were coerced or ordered to shave off their mustaches. The evil that is facial hair was virtually eradicated on the ESPN networks during that time . . . virtually. Somehow I managed to win the battle and triumph over this mustache persecution. For twenty-four years at ESPN I wore a mustache. To this day I am not sure how I kept both my job and my mustache.

The reason for this mustache hatred at ESPN is also still a mystery to me. Little light was shed on this in the attempts by ESPN "suits" to get me to lose my facial hair. In one of these verbal sparring sessions I was told that it was not appropriate for me to have a mustache. I asked why. Channeling his inner Eric Hoffer, the ESPN executive said to me, "Because sportscasters don't have mustaches." I pointed out that I had been a national sportscaster for almost six years at that point, and I most certainly did have a mustache. So it seemed his logic was somewhat flawed. Sticking with his "the Earth is flat" approach he said, "That doesn't mean I am wrong." Hmm.

Given the scarcity of facial hair on our public servants and politicians, the old canard that people with mustaches are perceived as somehow less trustworthy may still have a place in our society. That may have influenced ESPN. I certainly had girlfriends during that period that had trust issues with me, but I don't think the mustache was the reason. As for the viewers, well, I doubt a mustache made them less inclined to trust me when I told them Pernell Whitaker was a defensive genius or Mike Tyson viewed the Marquis of Queensberry rules as merely "guidelines."

The ESPN facial hair ban lasted well into the early 2000s. Now, however, we see many ESPN personalities with facial hair. Tony Kornheiser, for instance, has both mustache and beard. That clearly puts to rest the argument that you can't trust a sportscaster with facial hair. Tony is practically the reincarnation of Edward R. Murrow—well, except for the masks, costumes, and buffoonery, and the frivolous factual misstatements . . . other than that, he's just like Murrow.

In 2006 both my mustache and I had been at Showtime Networks for two years when this little story took an ironic turn. One evening while trimming the mustache, I made a slip, and by the time I was done "fixing" it I looked like a cross between Adolph Hitler and Thomas Dewey. My wife heard my shrieks of horror and rushed into the bathroom to see if I had cut myself or, worse yet, had once again broken a bathroom fixture. Relieved that is was neither of those catastrophes, she helped me make the only sane decision left to me . . . cut off the mustache. Once I did she looked at my face and, based on her expression, I could read her mind: "Wow, I'd rather he broke the fixture."

I remember thinking at the time that I should call that ESPN executive and say, "*Now* are you happy?" Then I realized he wasn't at ESPN anymore and I didn't know at what small market station he might work.

I did end up doing several *Showtime Championship Boxing* shows without my mustache. Amazingly, during that time span the world kept spinning on its axis, the Israelis and Arabs still hated each other, Madonna reinvented herself one more time, and Bobby Knight was still a jerk. In other words, the universe seemed relatively unaffected by me appearing on national television without a mustache. Go figure.

In case you were waiting for the ironic turn, here it is. While on a plane ride with Showtime Executive Producer David Dinkins Jr., he asked me, "Are you going to grow your mustache back?" David does not often ask frivolous questions, so I rightfully took that as a nudge to grow it back, and I did. Over a period of twenty-four years ESPN

Here I am working at ringside for Showtime Networks, still sporting my mustache, a couple of decades after ESPN executives tried to get me to shave it off. My mustache survived the dark days of facial hair tyranny at ESPN. The mustaches of many of my ESPN comrades were less fortunate. They fell to the razors of their oppressors. (Photo by Tom Casino/Showtime)

executives could not talk me into shaving off the mustache, but with one tiny hint from my boss at Showtime I was convinced to grow it back.

So, I soldier on with my mustache, hoping against hope it won't prevent me from sustaining a reasonably long sportscasting career. Oh, I just remembered, I do know where that ESPN executive can be found. He's actually in the major market city of Philadelphia, where I hear he's really learning to enjoy automobile sales.

Getting Respect
Is Not Always Easy

Sometimes life definitely imitates art. With Rodney Dangerfield such was the case on almost every occasion I interacted with this enjoyable and quirky man.

Just as his famous catch phrase indicated, he was a person concerned about getting "No Respect." From the first time I met him, the night before the 1985 Marvin Hagler-Tommy Hearns fight, I knew him as a vulnerable person who was down-to-earth and, quite frankly, worried about almost everything.

He and I were sitting in his Caesars Palace dressing room one night after his show, and he was having a completely rhetorical discussion with himself about whether he should accept an invitation to go on the *David Letterman Show*. He was more than a little worried that Letterman, known to treat some guests less hospitably, would turn his acerbic humor on Rodney. "It's his show, his turf, he controls everything, and I could look really bad. What if he thinks I'm too square?"

At the time Rodney was in huge demand, not only with casinos in Las Vegas and Atlantic City, but also on college campuses as a comedian and speaker. He was also starring in movies. With all that going in his favor, I found it intriguing that he should be so worried about whether he even took the Letterman offer to guest. He talked himself in and out of accepting the guest shot about six times as the evening wore on and we had moved to a nearby cocktail lounge.

He apparently did talk himself into the appearance—he would go on the *Letterman* show in 1986 and things went quite well. He brought his own top ten list along—it was very funny—and promoted his movie *Back to School*. And more importantly Letterman was as nice as could be, showing, well, the proper respect.

Some would suggest that putting these worries into the atmosphere might end up providing self-fulfilling prophecies. The more new age thinkers among us might argue that a man who spent at least 250 nights a year on stage saying "I don't get no respect," might actually make it so, but I can't say for sure,

My favorite Rodney story is the ultimate in life imitating art. In the late 1980s I was doing a pay-per-view telecast in Madison Square Garden and we were only about five minutes away from going on the air. I was on my mark to go on camera at the top of the show with my broadcast partner when I noticed out of the corner of my eye a little commotion to my left. It was Rodney Dangerfield, who I was slated to have a drink with after the fight, talking to a slightly ruffled pair of ushers. It wasn't hard to figure out from the gestures and body language that they were indicating to Rodney that his seat was taken and they did not have another one for him. I knew immediately what was happening. Rodney had a "promoter's ticket" that gives you a seat in a front row, but without an assigned seat. If there is some small mistake and too many are given out, and/or you are late, as Rodney was, you can have a problem. So, this big star was being told he did not have a seat—and in this packed house, there were no other ones for the eye to see at that late moment. This could have been a *Saturday Night Live* satire on Rodney Dangerfield getting "no respect." The problem was, it was really happening.

It was just about to become a major embarrassment when I took my earpiece off and started over to where they were having the ruckus. At this point the stage manager was loudly imploring me to get back, because we were only about two minutes from going on the air. I went over, grabbed Rodney, and took him to ringside where I told the stage manager to give Rodney his chair. I jumped back to my spot, got wired up again for the show, and got my earpiece on just in time to hear an apoplectic producer counting down five . . . four . . . three . . . and a few seconds later I greeted the world to this live pay-per-view telecast.

Rodney stayed at ringside with me the whole night, passing me notes and making jokes off microphone that had me suppressing laughs, all the while trying to concentrate on doing my job. The stage manager was none too happy about having to squat down for the evening—but Rodney gave him two tickets to the concert he was doing the next night in the New York area, and that more than placated him. Free tickets can win you affection, if not respect.

In the late 1980s for almost a year I did a weekly stage show at Caesars Palace right near the race and sports book, called *Boxing by the Book*. I introduced clips from great Caesars Palace fights, interviewed boxing celebrities, and started each show off with a song parody about the week in boxing or the guest that evening. It became a hangout for some interesting folks from show business including Telly Savalas, Jack Klugman, Steve Rossi, and my friend Rodney—who performed at Caesars often during that period.

One night we had a full house and I looked in the back and standing there was Rodney, who had wandered down from his hotel room to catch the show—in his bathrobe and slippers. At one point he even bantered with me from the audience, so I introduced him, of course, and then the whole crowd realized he was there in his bathrobe no less. They broke out in huge applause, and his attire raised no eyebrows. Hey, it was the 80s in Las Vegas—nothing seemed taboo.

I always thought it ironic that on stage Rodney controlled what happened and almost never failed. Off stage, where no one can really control things, his life had its share of rough patches, even with his great successes. To me though, there was one constant, he was a man who always deserved respect.

Advice Can Be Both Right and Wrong at the Same Time

The late Don Dunphy, who you met in chapter 4, once said to me, "The best advice I can give you as a sportscaster is to remember, when you are on the air, it's not about you." What he was essentially saying is, never make yourself bigger than the event you are covering. That advice is absolutely right . . . and it is absolutely wrong.

Even though it was advice given in 1986, it remains correct in 2012 when it comes to doing your job properly and best serving the viewers of your telecast. However, it is totally wrong in 2012 as advice to a sportscaster on the best way to get ahead in the industry. If Don were still alive I am sure he would agree with me when I say that the majority of sportscasters working today believe it is *always* about them. Amazingly they do so with the endorsement and even encouragement of their networks or stations and their producers. We live in a time when most networks value argument over discussion, opinion over information, and loudness over intelligence. A seismic shift has taken place in sports broadcasting in the last fifteen years. Behavior that was once considered inappropriate at best, is now not only tolerated, but encouraged.

Here I should digress (not the first time in this book), and tell you that there are a handful of topics in life that I am so passionate about that I could never learn enough about them or discuss them in too much detail. There is horseback riding (and all things western), music, theater, and finally sportscasting. My interest in those topics knows no bounds. While the first three are avocations, sportscasting is my raison d'être. There is nothing about it or sports television in general that does not interest me. I devour all information pertaining to it. I dissect every show I do, and most that I watch. While I don't take myself too seriously (as much of this book shows), I do take sportscasting very seriously.

That digression is intended to assure you that my claim that sportscasting has changed dramatically (not for the better) is not some idle statement or some sentimental bromide about the "good old days." It is a well-considered assessment of my profession.

I am hardly known as a combative personality, and I have steadfastly refused to criticize my colleagues over the years. So, even writing this chapter is out of character for me. In stories written about me, my public persona has been described with phrases such as "cuddly," "eternally amiable," and "terminally agreeable." So, I'm not exactly a guy that's out there looking for controversy. I hope that reputation will give my words in this chapter even more meaning.

The changes I am talking about in sports broadcasting have affected both of the two major areas in sports television—in-studio shows and live remote telecasts. First, let's consider the studio shows that dot the landscape not just at ESPN, but other networks as well. My alma mater, ESPN, likes to call itself the sports leader, and unfortunately this is one area where it has most assuredly been the leader. I should point out, however, it is certainly not the only offender.

Consider this, in a recent book about ESPN's history it was revealed that in 2001, a high-ranking ESPN executive asked for the development of a show that featured "two guys yelling at each other." Think about that. He did not ask for a show where two guys were giving great analysis, or being glib and humorous, or even having a clever debate. He wanted a show with two guys yelling at each other. The show that resulted was *Pardon the Interruption*. This was the beginning of that executive and others shaping ESPN into an opinion- and personality-driven operation that valued "disagreement and argument" above all else.

I was still at ESPN when all this happened, and the change was palpable. While *Sportscenter* anchors were already free to offer plenty of opinion and snide humor in the middle of reporting the news, this development sent ESPN careening even more in a less-information-and-more-opinion-based direction. ESPN management made it mandatory that there be debate in virtually every segment of every studio show—even if that disagreement had to be manufactured, which it often was. Now, more than a decade later, argument for its own sake is a way of life at the network I called home for twenty-four years. With the exception of some journalistic bastions like *Outside the Lines* on television and *The Sporting Life* on ESPN radio, there is little room for a show that is not totally opinion or personality driven.

Having said all that, I can assure you I like to hear interesting opinions and debate on television, and I get a kick out of larger-than-life personalities. I like them when they are genuine, not manufactured. I like humor when it is not painfully orchestrated and sophomoric, when it doesn't rely on props, when it doesn't demean a subject or person just for the sake of it. I like humor when it adds to instead of subtracts from the topic at hand. To be fair, there is still some humor at ESPN that comes organically out of a moment. But, that brand is greatly outnumbered by the sophomoric humor embedded in the system to go along with the equally sophomoric faux conflict. I'm not suggesting that all humor in sports broadcasting needs to be on the Billy Crystal level, but occasionally I'd like something above Pauly Shore.

At ESPN there are two sets of standards for sportscasters contributing to studio shows. The first applies to the *Sportscenter* anchors and hosts of their own shows are encouraged to be as freewheeling as they would like. You can add to that group analysts on shows and segments where they are supposed to deliver the outrageous more often than the valid. Sometimes these segments have titles to them that actually direct the analysts to be so subjective as to defy logic or analysis.

Meanwhile the second set of standards applies to another group of sportscasters at ESPN who work under the closest of journalistic scrutiny. That would be the reporters who work for *Sportscenter* and some of the studio shows.

I understand this dynamic because among the many roles I filled at ESPN over twenty-four years was *Sportscenter* reporter. In that role you rightfully operate under strict guidelines where your every word is scrutinized by news producers and editors. There was, and it appears still is, a diligent effort by all concerned to make sure the stories are reported as news stories—both accurate and fair. The vetting of these stories back at ESPN's headquarters in Bristol, Connecticut is exacting. Scripts are submitted for approval, and reporters are often questioned about anything that smacks of editorializing or factual misstatement.

I often covered major league baseball games on Saturday and Sunday for *Sportscenter*, a weekend baseball show, *ESPN News*, and any other network ESPN might have launched on any given week. One particular game, involving the Seattle Mariners in the final weekend of the season, sticks out in my mind. It was well into the evening when we finally filed our last report on a Seattle loss that kept them in a tailspin and put their playoff hopes in jeopardy. It was a difficult and sensitive story to cover fairly, but we felt good about the fact that it detailed the M's failure, but did so in an evenhanded fashion. I went back to the hotel with my producer and we watched in horror as the *Sportscenter* anchor introduced the story with several snide jokes at the Mariners' expense, and then spent some time editorializing about them choking, before finally leading to our story.

Needless to say, when we went to the ballpark the next day, none of the Mariners or their team personnel noticed so much that our story was fair. No, they were preoccupied with the cheap imitation of Don Rickles that the *Sportscenter* anchor had done. This was not the only time this happened to me when working in the field as a reporter for ESPN. I can only presume many other *Sportscenter* reporters have experienced the same thing.

A psychiatrist would diagnose *Sportscenter* as having an extreme case of dissocial personality disorder, better known to all of us as a split personality. The diligent efforts to monitor what the reporters do and the resulting stories demonstrate the excellent reporting ESPN is capable of producing. Then, when things go back to the studio, the dark side of the network takes over, where the "it's all about me" mentality kicks in for many anchors and analysts alike. Seeing these two approaches side by side is like looking at a revitalized urban neighborhood only a block away from one that is not.

As I mentioned earlier, ESPN is not the only offender, but it provided the blueprint for others to follow. Analysts on football, basketball, and baseball studio shows on other networks and channels provide the same faux debate and lowbrow humor that has now become an industry standard. And, often the commentary is so mean-spirited and personal that it reminds me of how I acted as a ten-year-old watching that baseball game. Perhaps their fathers never gave them the lecture I got. Or worse, maybe they do know better, but need to get ahead so badly they will go over the line to do it.

If many studio analysts are guilty of the "I'll do anything to be noticed" mentality, a good number of analysts working on live sports events have taken that approach to a whole new level. At least the studio analysts and hosts are not diverting the viewer's attention from a live event so they can be noticed. For my colleagues doing live sporting events, the "me first" approach requires them to hijack an event. They have that pesky game, contest, or match taking the viewer's attention away from them. And wouldn't you know it, that event sometimes gets in the way of what *they* want to say. How tragic.

There was a time when the producer of a live event would chastise announcers for spending too much time talking about something that does not correlate in some way to what's going on in the event. This is especially true in a sport like boxing, where the whole event can change in an instant. Based on what I often see on television, it doesn't seem many producers are trying to rein in these rogue sportscasters. Worse yet, I suspect the producers, and the networks they work for, are encouraging all this.

We have seen many major boxing matches, for instance, where three sportscasters are debating amongst themselves something only vaguely related to the match we are all watching. This debate has been known to extend for almost an entire three-minute round, while the action in the ring goes virtually unnoticed by these intrepid communicators.

Mind you, I appreciate clever asides and fun interaction between sportscasters during an event. Anyone who ever listened to me commentating boxing with Barry Tompkins from 1988 to 1995 on ESPN would attest to the fact that humor was a staple of our repertoire. I believe we advanced that art form. I can tell you that we *never* did it at the expense of the fighters or took over the event. And we never failed to chronicle what was happening in the ring.

Barry Tompkins remembers it this way: "Things struck us funny and we added humor, but we never shirked our responsibility to the fights. We walked that fine line and that's hard to do. The ESPN executives let us freelance and have some fun because they weren't really invested enough in the show to get upset." That was before the "it's all about me" crowd had taken over, so there were still people at ESPN who worried about paying attention to the live event. I'm not sure the ESPN decision makers would even recognize the humorous parts of these *Top Rank Boxing Shows* if they saw them now—no masks, no props, and no fake arguments. Now, I'm not suggesting we were the reincarnation of Noel Coward, but compared to what passes for humor on sports networks today, well, maybe we were close.

Barry's broadcasting philosophy mirrors mine. "Announcers should not be bigger than the event. We are the chroniclers of the event." Ironically, before becoming a sportscaster Barry was a musical performer in a band that toured the country. Barry is a self-educated, self-made journalist, and he is a better one than most of the "yuk it up" guys now on the air who often came from prestigious journalism schools.

In most sports the action is regimented and you are forced to follow some kind of format. I have done play-by-play on a number of other sports including basketball, and those sports keep you to a pattern and require certain things of the play-by-play announcer and the analyst. Even so many announcers, especially analysts, somehow find the time to "chew the scenery" and take us away from the event. In boxing, where it is more free form, it's even easier for sportscasters to go off on flights of fancy—boxing is the worst sport in which to do that. If you get caught up in a long story or opinion that is off topic, you can obliterate the moment of a single punch or flurry that ends the contest or changes it dramatically. You don't need a master's degree in broadcasting from Northwestern to figure that out—it's just common sense.

Perhaps the tone for all of this was set many years ago by the guru of "notice me" sportscasting—Howard Cosell. It's true that Cosell helped bring a broader view of the world into sportscasting, and for that he should be lauded. It is also true, however, that his celebrity allowed him to make any event as much about him as it was about the participants. Who else but Cosell could have taken events involving the biggest personality of them all, Muhammad Ali, and still make us notice Howard more?

The perfect example of that was the second Ali-Leon Spinks fight. Ali had been mostly outboxing Spinks for the first thirteen rounds of the fight. Winning the title back would be a historic feat, which at the time might have been the crowning touch on Ali's career. A sportscaster in that position might reasonably be expected to build the drama by weaving into the commentary the importance of that with facts or anecdotes linked to the achievement, while still leaving open the possibility of an ever-desperate Spinks finding a way to stop Ali, or cut him, or create multiple knockdowns that could still win him a decision. A sportscaster in that position would not reasonably be expected to take up much of the 14th round reciting the lyrics of the Bob Dylan song "Forever Young," completely ignoring what was happening in the ring. That, however, is exactly what Howard did. Really, he did that.

Some may see what Howard did as a bold and creative way of paying homage to Ali. I see it as the single most egregious act of ego ever displayed by a sportscaster. He stole one of boxing's most historic moments for shameless self-aggrandizement. So, Howard Cosell was likely the forefather of the "me first" approach to sportscasting.

An offshoot of all this (also something taken to great heights by Cosell) is the use of opinion to replace analysis. There is a distinction, even if many producers and sports executives don't understand that. Analyst is after all part of the title of sports analyst. That's the title of the person sitting next to the host or play-by-play announcer. The title is not "opinion giver" or "mass opinion shaper." Opinions may be part of some types of analysis, but pure opinion is never to be confused with analysis. Using opinion under the guise of calling it analysis is often the sign that a color commentator is too lazy to do the homework necessary to provide real analysis. Anyone can have an opinion on anything. Providing a well-informed opinion requires offering analysis to go with it.

Analysis is using knowledge of an athlete or team to explain something that has just happened or foreshadow something that might happen. It might be a statistic, a fact you learned about the athlete or team's preparation for the event, a comment by someone involved with the event, or a trend in performance. All those things can help the viewer understand something in a sporting event. Not all of them involve or lead to opinions. Sometimes they do, but if they do, it will offer the viewer an opinion that is reinforced with information the viewer does not have at his or her disposal. *That* is the analyst's job!

Both analysts in studio and (especially) at live events have come to rely on opinions instead of analysis, and television executives and even fans have been willing to accept it. Commentators in all sports feel free to simply pass judgment on an athlete for certain behavior or second-guess athletes or teams without putting it in the proper perspective. Just having participated in a sport or being considered an expert does not give you the right to do nothing but blurt out opinions to us as viewers. More than that is required from an analyst on a sporting event. We are all paid handsomely to do more.

Sportscasters (both play-by-play and analysts) have the obligation to give fans information before they ever provide opinions. To me this is a golden rule of sportscasting, one that has become completely lost in the cacophony of opinions, debate, and posturing that has enveloped sportscasting. Sportscasters are supposed to be armed with knowledge and facts that the fans at home don't have. That is what they need to convey and utilize to inform the viewer and analyze the event. A sportscaster who does his or her homework and does not want to steal the spotlight for self-aggrandizement will always put those things first before pontificating.

Here's the kicker to all this: The man I quoted at the beginning, Don Dunphy, was no shrinking violet when it came to self-confidence. His son Bob, who you also met in chapter 4, said of Don: "My dad had an ego. He liked being on television and all that went with it." This statement is not at odds with Don's advice that once you are on the air "it's not about you." In fact, when Don passed away, his *New York Times* obituary said, "Mr. Dunphy was an objective voice in a subjective sport." Your ego should drive you to succeed, not just to be noticed.

There are still many talented play-by-play announcers, hosts, and analysts on television who serve the viewer as they should and who heed Don's code of conduct. Unfortunately, they are now greatly outnumbered. Because I am listening carefully I can hear you asking, "Why don't you name the current offenders?" Here's my idea: you watch the next month of sports television with this chapter in mind and you will name them yourselves. Won't that be more fun?

Revisiting History
Is Enlightening and Fun

It may surprise some of you to know that I am not a boxing historian, even though I play one on TV. No, really, I am not a true historian. My Showtime colleague Steve Farhood . . . now *there* is a historian. Steve could probably tell you who Rocky Marciano took to the senior prom, where the prom was held, and what kind of flowers were included in the wrist corsage The Rock gave his date. OK, I'm exaggerating; he might not know the flowers.

Steve knows much more about boxing history than me. Although I do know more about old television westerns than him, so I think that makes us even. I do, however, love boxing history and I know more about it than the average Joe. Actually I know more than the average Frank as well . . . not sure about the average Bill though . . . Bills are pretty knowledgeable. I digress, again. The point I'm attempting to make is that I am a devotee of boxing history, but I defer to some of my colleagues when it comes to the title historian.

All that being said, I love to write and talk about boxing's past. The history of the sport is so colorful and interesting. I was privileged to get to write and host an ESPN show called *Big Fights Boxing Hour*. We did twenty-six episodes and I am as proud of that show as anything I have done in television. As an offshoot of that I also did dozens of historical commentaries/essays for a number of years on ESPN. I still get letters and e-mails from people about these—and they still often pop up on ESPN's large family of channels.

ESPN controls when these commentaries surface on their networks, but here I am free to run amok with essays. So, I thought I would share some of them with you in this book. Since I wrote this book very much in my own voice, I suspect that's how you are reading it. Well, keep doing that in this chapter, and then you can "hear" me reading these essays. I am assuming that if you bought this book and made it to chapter nine, you must like the way I deliver things on television, so you won't mind imagining me delivering these essays. But, if you want to imagine someone like, oh, I don't know . . . maybe James Earl Jones delivering them, I won't fight you. He's quite a narrator, and he's Darth Vader, so that trumps everything. Just please don't cheat on me and imagine another boxing announcer delivering these. I'd hate to show my jealous side.

In any case, taken collectively these essays give you a pretty good idea of how I see the history of boxing. They will give you a glimpse into what fascinates and inspires me about the great boxing figures of the past. I have selected some of my favorites from the dozens that I did. I loved writing these. I hope you enjoy reading them.

JACK JOHNSON

Jack Johnson was a larger-than-life figure. He had to be to persevere as a black heavyweight champion in the early 1900s. Remember that the heavyweight title was the most coveted prize in sports back then, and many Americans could not accept that a black man held the title. So, clearly Johnson's impact transcended the boxing ring. He was a catalyst for hate on the one hand and hope on the other. His every achievement in life was either diminished or exaggerated, depending on who was interpreting those achievements.

Many white journalists were appalled that he had marriages with white women, and so they exaggerated reports of his womanizing and portrayed him as an immoral character. And, as a boxer, they were loathe to give him the credit he deserved, as evidenced by the way they built up aging challenger James Jeffries who came out of retirement to fight Johnson. To his supporters, many of them black, Johnson offered so much hope that he was something of a god. Many deeds in the ring and all the acts of defiance against white society were embellished, often beyond truth.

With all this as the backdrop, the myths surrounding Johnson almost obscure the remarkable facts. Forgetting all the social turmoil that swirled around him, and the theatrical flare with which he lived his life, there is one basic truth that remains unchallenged—he was the best prizefighter of his era, and one of the best of all time. His skills were light-years ahead of most opponents. If that boxing legacy were all he left behind, he would still be considered an extraordinary athlete. But, when you throw in all the rest, well, you have an extraordinary man as well.

JACK DEMPSEY

Sometimes an athlete not only helps define the times he lives in, but belongs in that era body and soul. Such a man was Jack Dempsey. Such a time was the roaring 20s.

In that era two athletes, Dempsey and Babe Ruth, meant more than any others. In fact they meant more than almost anyone. A case in point—once Ruth was asked by a reporter if it seemed wrong that he made more money each year than the president of the United States. Ruth replied simply, "No, I had a better year than him."

Dempsey ascended to the heavyweight throne in 1919 by beating Jess Willard. This itinerant miner and fruit picker had entered boxing with bravado and a free-swinging style that fit the times. He was also a gregarious and fun-loving public figure.

Dempsey was not the most active heavyweight champion, with only six defenses in his seven-year title reign, but all his matches were big events that created boxing folklore. His battle with George Carpentier produced the first million-dollar gate in boxing with 80,000 fans on hand. His fight with Tommy Gibbons bankrupted a Montana town, and 102,000 people came to Soldier Field in Chicago to see Dempsey's rematch with Gene Tunney. That throng witnessed the infamous long-count controversy.

No fight defines Dempsey better than his 1923 match with Argentine Luis Firpo. He knocked down Firpo seven times in two rounds, but hit the canvas twice himself. Once Jack was knocked through the ropes into a row of newspaper reporters who simply shoved him back in the ring. Firpo finally stayed down in round 2, another victim of The Manassa Mauler. Never was a nickname more apt. Jack Dempsey was a larger-than-life figure in a time tailored to his talents and personality.

SONNY LISTON

If you think that Mike Tyson invented that menacing stare during prefight instructions that froze opponents with fear, well, you are wrong. Tyson may have used it to good effect, but the man who invented it was Charles "Sonny" Liston.

He was the monster of the heavyweight division in the late 1950s and early '60s, capable of mayhem both inside and outside the ring. After a poor and troubled beginning in life as one of twenty-four children in first rural Arkansas and then the rough streets of St. Louis, Liston would twice end up in prison. His second sentence interrupted his pro boxing career, but when he got out in 1958 he went on a four-year spree in which he decimated the heavyweight division. He won nineteen matches—sixteen by knockout. Only Eddie Machen and Bert Whitehurst (who did it twice) were able to go the distance with him.

While Floyd Patterson held the heavyweight title, Liston was the most feared man in the division. He would, of course, win the title, intimidating and beating Patterson twice, further adding to his image as a larger-than-life bully. Lost in all this is the fact that Liston was a very skilled fighter with an accurate and thunderous jab. He was not a brawler, but rather a measured puncher with brutal power.

While there is no denying his dark side outside the ring, over the years I have talked to many people who knew him well and they insist that if treated with respect, Sonny was a good and loyal friend. And, they say, he was capable of kindness that belied his public image. He preferred to hide that not only from the public, but also from his opponents—which made that prefight stare all the more effective.

JOE FRAZIER

(THE EARLY DAYS)

When twenty-one-year-old Olympic Gold Medalist Joe Frazier turned pro in 1965, he had a group of investors called "Cloverlay" backing him on the business front, and in the ring he had the help of great trainer Yank Durham. It was a formidable team that propelled this young Philadelphian on the fast track to heavyweight contention.

With Joe's blue-collar work ethic guiding them, they set up an ambitious fight schedule that ultimately had Joe boxing thirteen times in the first year and a half of his pro career. While the brash young heavyweight champion Muhammad Ali was stealing headlines in more ways than one, Frazier was amassing knockout wins and delighting fans with his aggressive hell-bent-for-leather style. And, he was beating good heavyweights like Oscar Bonavena.

The heavyweight division was an interesting place under Ali with holdovers like Eddie Machen, Floyd Patterson, and Zora Folley still in the mix, and young lions like Frazier and Jerry Quarry on the rise. It was Frazier who was on the verge of taking over when Ali had his three-year exile from boxing for his refusal to serve in the military.

From 1965 to his first epic match with Ali, Frazier was a wrecking machine—destroying any heavyweight in his path. In that time he won twenty-six fights—all but three by knockout. In that time he beat Oscar Bonavena (twice), Quarry, Machen, George Chuvalo, Jimmy Ellis, the undefeated Buster Mathis, and light heavyweight champ Bob Foster. He brought zeal to the sport that was fun to watch in the ring. His hard work and undeniable courage showed in every fight, and ultimately those two attributes would provide much of the Frazier boxing legacy.

JOE FRAZIER

(ANALYSIS OF HIS STYLE)

Joe Frazier's greatness will always be partially hidden under Muhammad Ali's shadow. That may be one of the most unfortunate facts in all of sports. In his prime, Frazier was as much a textbook example of his fighting style as Ali was of his own. That's why, together, they could create what amounts to the near perfect boxing match.

Some have said that Joe's style was one-dimensional. They have it all wrong. It was a style filled with nuance—a head fake, jab your way in, double left hook, and another body shot to top it off. And within those moves were many variations on the theme. Through determination and hard work Frazier turned aggression into an art form. To beat him you had to be the perfect boxer with a great chin—Ali was that. Or, you had to be unimaginably powerful—George Foreman was that. In most other time periods it is quite possible Frazier might never have lost. So, while there's no denying Ali his legacy, we should never let it obscure the greatness of Joe Frazier.

MUHAMMAD ALI

(DRIVE TO A SECOND TITLE)

We use many adjectives to describe Muhammad Ali, but one that is underused is resiliency.

In 1971, after his epic loss to Joe Frazier, the twenty-nine-year-old Ali had already been through the turmoil of his refusal to enter the draft, a three-year exile from boxing, and the disappointment of the Frazier loss. And yet, four months after the Frazier fight he would embark on a three-and-a-half-year, fourteen-fight odyssey to regain the heavyweight title. He would win thirteen of those matches, but suffer a broken jaw in the one loss to Ken Norton. Along the way he beat the likes of Jerry Quarry, George Chuvalo, Bob Foster, Norton in the rematch, and finally Frazier in another pitched battle. All that finally got him, at age thirty-two, a title shot with George Foreman.

The climb back to the top was accomplished with hard work and a brutal fight schedule against tough opponents. So, go ahead and call Ali flashy, call him flamboyant, but please also note that he was resilient.

SUGAR RAY LEONARD

(THE EARLY DAYS)

When Sugar Ray Leonard turned pro in February of 1977 he was already an Olympic Gold medalist and a national hero. From that moment to his title shot against Wilfred Benitez, Leonard was on a carefully orchestrated march through boxing journeymen and one-time contenders designed to prepare him for his coronation. The mastermind behind the creation of Sugar Ray, the professional, was the wily Angelo Dundee, who had previously taken another Olympic champion, Muhammad Ali, on this same journey. No trainer/manager in boxing history has been as good at picking the right opponents for his fighter as Dundee.

In the twenty-five professional fights that preceded the Benitez fight, Leonard face brawlers, boxers, lefties, counter punchers, lightweights coming up in weight, and middleweights coming down in weight. Most were veterans just barely past their primes, and others were youngsters not yet as good as they might become. In short, it was a smorgasbord of fighters Dundee thought Leonard could beat, but all designed to get him ready to be a champion.

So, when the fight was set with the masterful Benitez, there were more than a few boxing experts and fans who thought Leonard would prove to be more style than substance. They thought he was more a marketing creation than a great boxer, and they thought he was a protected fighter who would be exposed by Benitez. Dundee knew these people were wrong. Leonard was the real McCoy. He would become a great champion, produce some of the most exciting fights in the '80s, and help make that era one of boxing's best. The foundation for all that was laid in his rise to stardom in the late 1970s.

MARVIN HAGLER

(THE EARLY DAYS)

In the mid and late 1970s, middleweights on the eastern seaboard were a talented and tough-minded lot who fought each other regularly and dreamed of a world title shot. They were men like Bennie Briscoe, Bobby Watts, Willie "The Worm" Monroe, and Eugene Hart. And, there was the one who would in fact emerge as the best of them all, Marvelous Marvin Hagler. Well, back then he was just Marvin Hagler, but he was marvelous in the ring.

They were a fraternity of combatants who respected each other but battled fiercely. Hagler credits his long run as champion to the fact that he was more than battle tested by those fighters. At the time Briscoe, who did get two world title shots, was the one who many thought would be the star of the group. He fell just short, but Hagler took the mantle and wore it proudly in a six-year championship reign that included some of the most memorable fights in that or any other era.

As great as Hagler was as a middleweight champion, he's just as proud of the fact that he was able to stand tall among those terrific boxers he faced before arriving on the world stage.

TOMMY HEARNS

Emanuel Steward once described Tommy Hearns as the Elvis Presley of boxing. When Elvis hit the stage you weren't quite sure what would happen, but you knew it would be entertaining and exciting. That also sums up the career of Tommy Hearns. But for a few training glitches and tactical errors in the ring, he might have never lost a match.

Hearns had fifty-nine wins, including dominant ones over the likes of Roberto Duran, Wilfred Benitez, and Pipino Cuevas. Ironically it is the near misses against Sugar Ray Leonard and Marvin Hagler that define him to many boxing fans. At first blush that seems wrong, but maybe in retrospect it's not so bad. In his first match with Leonard, a 13th round TKO loss, they produced a classic match filled with ebb and flow. Their second meeting, years later, produced a slugfest that most believe Hearns won, despite the judges' ruling of a draw.

And what of the match with Hagler? It is widely thought of as the greatest three rounds in middleweight history. This match was a unique collision of skill and ferocity. Even in losing, Tommy Hearns showed us why, if there were moments when he played second fiddle to Leonard and Hagler, he still made sweet music—just like Elvis.

JAKE LAMOTTA

The great filmmaker John Huston once said that some people live lives while others, like him, live novels. Well, he could also have applied that phrase to Jake LaMotta.

From a reform school beginning, this tough kid from the Bronx won and lost fortunes, won and lost the affections of beautiful women, battled the mob, faced off with Congress, and saw his tumultuous life turned into the hit movie *Raging Bull*. Oh, and along the way he also managed to become the middleweight champion of the world.

It is perhaps that last fact that sometimes gets lost in the shuffle. To use the vernacular of his day, Jake was "one hell of a fighter." If Sugar Ray Robinson had never been born, LaMotta might be thought of as much for his prowess in the ring as his colorful life outside it. He fought Robinson six times, winning only once, and always being forced to exist in the shadow of the greatest fighter of all time. In his stand-up comic days LaMotta quipped, "I fought Sugar Ray so many times I almost got diabetes."

His other major rivalry proves just how good he was as a fighter. In 1943 and '44 he fought the great Hall of Famer Fritzie Zivic four times and won three of those battles.

Even in his greatest triumph he was robbed of legitimacy. When he beat Marcel Cerdan for the title, many felt it was because of a shoulder injury Cerdan suffered early in the match. LaMotta's chance to prove that his win was no fluke evaporated when Cerdan died in a plane crash before they could fight a planned rematch. This was yet another twist in the novel that was Jake LaMotta's life.

ETHNICITY IN BOXING

Boxing is a sport where people of many ethnic, religious, and racial backgrounds have found a way, for the most part, to function together. More than one sage boxing pundit has suggested that the only color that really matters in boxing is green. As important as money is to the sport, that might be a slight overstatement, but it does reflect the prevailing concept of what drives fighters, managers, promoters, and officials to work together to get the job done.

The irony of all this is that boxing is one of the few sports where ethnicity has been used as a means to an end. Boxing has always walked the fine line of promoting ethnic, racial, and nationalistic pride, while hoping it doesn't become too divisive.

In the earlier days of boxing, fans used their ethnic heroes as beacons of hope. Nowhere can we see how this benefited the sport more than the three-way rivalry between Tony Canzoneri, Barney Ross, and Jimmy McLarnin. These three Hall of Famers had fifteen fights involving each other in both the lightweight and welterweight divisions. Titles were exchanged back and forth, and huge gates were produced as Italian fans rooted for Canzoneri, Jews boosted Ross, and Irish fans supported McLarnin. Two of the Ross-McLarnin fights attracted crowds of 65,000 and 40,000 people.

Perhaps we look at these ethnic rivalries through a gauze-covered historical lens and see them as more benign than they were. But, they fueled the sport of boxing, and for the most part society came out unscathed by them.

When It Comes to Typecasting, You Can Run but You Can't Hide

I can tell you that I have announced college basketball on national television, I did a general sports radio show for years on an ESPN affiliate, I have covered a number of sports for *Sportscenter*, I have performed live on stage for thousands of people, and I have given dozens of speeches on topics ranging from sports to casino marketing. I can tell you all that until I am blue in the face, and most of you will still see me as a boxing announcer. Or, as people often say when they see me in the grocery store, "Hey, you're the boxing guy." Well, sometimes they also say, "Don't buy those bananas, they're too ripe." But that's not important.

The point I'm making is that it is a time-tested truth that once you are typecast by some measure of success, it is foolhardy to think you can alter that perception. It is a vexing problem for some people. I knew James Doohan who, of course, played Scotty in *Star Trek*. He came to some of the celebrity rodeos I participated in, and he told me of his days as a Shakespearean actor in England. That's right, Scotty was a Shakespearean actor. Admit it, you did not know that. I certainly didn't. I am a Trekkie, so I love James Doohan and his Scotty persona, but I don't have to live it. *He* was typecast.

I have a pretty eclectic set of interests, as you may have already guessed. So, there was a time when I resented the pigeonholing that being The Boxing Guy brought with it. Now, mind you, I like boxing and I love being a boxing announcer. So I did not want to run away from being a boxing announcer, I just wanted to do other things as well. I finally realized that for anyone in that situation, for that quest to be rewarding they can't expect to redefine how the public sees them. They simply have to enjoy these other endeavors. It took me a little while to figure that out.

Another bonus undeniable truth is that we all want to be something else. Actors wants to be directors, directors want to be actors, sportscasters want to be newscasters, newscasters want to be sportscasters, athletes want to be performers, performers want to be athletes, and everyone wants to be George Clooney. You get the idea. We all have fantasies floating around in our head, and some are attainable and some are not. Often we confuse the two.

The trick for any public figure is to understand just what you are capable of doing, so you can stretch out and do something different while not falling on your face. And you still have to understand that no matter how much you show you can do something else, 90 percent of the people who know you and your persona are still going to define you by whatever identity gained you acclaim. To 90 percent of you I am The Boxing Guy, which is why so much of this book has something to do with that sport. If I weren't The Boxing Guy I would never be doing this book. But it's also an undeniable truth that man does not live by boxing alone.

In the mid to late 1980s I was frustrated by the fact that I just couldn't convince the management at ESPN to give me more assignments in other sports. I had done a few, like work on NFL draft coverage, and cover some NBA playoffs, but the ESPN brass was very content for me to do only boxing. So, I took the only reasonable course of action, I decided to become a nightclub singer.

Hey, I loved to sing, had a good voice, had done a little performing in my previous life in Chicago, and I was kind of famous . . . so why not? OK, so maybe that thought process was a bit flawed, especially when you consider what I did next. In January of 1987 I got myself an engagement singing at Caesars Palace the weekend of the Marvin Hagler-Sugar Ray Leonard fight. What? Too high-profile for the first time? Yeah, maybe.

Several months earlier, Featherweight Champion Barry McGuigan's dad, a pub singer in Ireland, had entertained in the Olympic Lounge at Caesars the weekend his son fought there. It packed the place and got Caesars lots of publicity. When I suggested to Caesars executives that I could do that, they enthusiastically said yes. So, some three months later I would be making my nightclub and musical debut at Caesars Palace in Las Vegas.

That was all well and good, but no one at Caesars had bothered to ask me what exactly I was going to do on stage for two forty-five-minute shows over three nights. Good thing they didn't ask, because at that point I didn't have an act, I didn't have a band, and in short, I didn't have a clue. This should have made me terrified, but I was too excited and delusional to be terrified. I figured I would find an act and a band, and a clue. Well, I did. I had been introduced to a man named Tony Rome, who was a performer and then a manager of acts in Las Vegas. I called him up and said, "Let's have dinner. I'm doing a nightclub act at Caesars Palace the weekend of the Hagler-Leonard fight and I kind of need an act." He should have hung the phone up and run screaming into the night, but thankfully he didn't. Instead, he created an act for me and got the musicians to make it work. Well, there you are, nothing to worry about.

The week before the fight I came out to Las Vegas to rehearse with the three fine musicians who would back me and try very hard to keep me from ruining a perfectly good musical booking. We sequestered ourselves at a rehearsal space somewhere out in the desert. I was 100 percent focused on this musical act, but the sports broadcasting world wanted me for its needs. During that week leading up to the Hagler-Leonard fight, while I was rehearsing in the desert, my phone was ringing off the hook back in Chicago and at my hotel room in Las Vegas. I had calls from radio shows that wanted to interview me about the fight. I had over one hundred messages from radio stations all over the United States, in every major market. I ignored every message. I had precious little time to learn two forty-five-minute shows, and I was determined to get it right.

One day while we were rehearsing, the man who owned this facility came to me and said, "You have a phone call." A phone call? No one knew where I was. Hell, I didn't even know where I was. Out of curiosity I went to the phone. The voice on the other end said, "Hi, Mr.

Bernstein, this is Jim Rome, and I do a radio show in Santa Barbara and I would like to have you as a guest on my show." (Yes, *that* Jim Rome.) I had managed to hide from all these shows in major media markets in the United States. Here was a very young guy, who I certainly had never heard of, from a tiny station in Santa Barbara, who managed to track me down two days before the big fight. He had confidently, but courteously, asked me to be a guest. I laughed, and told him that even though I had no time to guest on his show, I *would* guest on his show, simply because anyone who had the resourcefulness to find me should be rewarded.

This story tells you all you need to know about why Jim became a multimedia superstar. His is an amazing success story, born out of a strong will to succeed. I did the interview with him that afternoon and it became obvious to me that day that he was a really good interviewer. That led to my frequent guest spots with Jim on his small station, and he later told me that the management there could not understand how he had managed to get me as a "regular" in such a small market. I have been interviewed by maybe a thousand people on television and radio, and I can tell you that none has done it better than Jim. He is one of the best sports interviewers I have ever seen. Ironically, at the writing of this book, Jim has joined CBS and Showtime, which delights me, because we are now teammates again.

So, Jim Rome pierced my armor of invisibility the week of the Hagler-Leonard fight, and after that interview I went back to rehearsing. Before I could say, "What I have gotten myself into," opening night was upon me.

This was no normal opening night. You see I had to do an ESPN Boxing show that night—our seventh anniversary *Top Rank Boxing Show*. And, it was outdoors in the same arena where the Hagler-Leonard fight would be. So, on a cold and drizzly night I used my voice announcing a two-and-a-half-hour boxing show. Not really the best prelude to your first important singing engagement.

That night, all through the casino, electricity seemed to surge through the air and the people. Two nights before the big fight and Las Vegas was alive with excitement. Before I knew it, I was up on stage singing in front of a star-studded audience at the Olympic lounge. All the press coverage and the buzz about it had everyone curious to see what I was going to do. I glided through the first two numbers and got a very good reception. I could see an almost palpable relief for most of the audience members, who were rooting for me to succeed. I remember looking at actor Victor French, the co-star of the television show *Little House on the Prairie*. I saw him applaud after the second number, lean back in his chair, and give me a nod of approval. OK, so now at least everybody knew I wasn't going to be terrible.

About five songs into the show there was a quintessential 1980s moment that was astonishing, even for those freewheeling and decadent times. I was singing one of the song parodies that had been written for me. I was scanning the audience to see a diverse group of people reacting to the funny lyrics that changed the George Gershwin tune "S'Marvelous" into a humorous ode to Marvelous Marvin Hagler. Here was John Madden at a table to my left, Gil Clancy, Tim Ryan, and Bob Arum a few tables over, to their right Tommy Hearns and Emanuel Steward, then Rodney Dangerfield at a stage side table. Toward the back, whom did I spy, but Ron Jeremy, famous porn star of the '80s hanging out with some of his stunning co-stars. My gaze was fixated a little too long on *that* table—I almost forgot the words to the song. Then the real distraction came when I looked down at a table just off the stage with a boxing notable. He had his head down near the table, and as he lifted it up he revealed a rolled-up hundred-dollar bill in his hand and on the table a half-snorted line of cocaine so long that Ron Jeremy could measure it against his . . . well, you get the idea. I stared down in amazement as I somehow continued to sing my song. He just looked up at me, smiled, and winked.

So, we know that this boxing personality had fun regardless of what I did on stage. But, the rest of the audience, who only had alcohol to make them happy, also seemed to enjoy the show. I did standards and special material, and perhaps because no one, maybe including me, knew what to expect, well the expectations were exceeded. The response was very nice.

The room was filled with sportswriters from all over the country who were there covering the fight. Many had already done items or stories in advance about my foray into the musical world, so they were there to see firsthand what this would turn out to be. The next day George Kimball wrote in the *Boston Herald*, "Al Bernstein, the ESPN commentator, opened to rave reviews this weekend as the headline act at the Olympic Lounge at Caesars Palace. While he did not outdraw Frank Sinatra, who was performing at the Golden Nugget a few miles down the strip, Bernstein played to a packed house all weekend and was amazingly good in launching his newest career." That was pretty much the way it went with items that sportswriters put in the newspapers during and after this engagement. And, really, when you think of it, who is more qualified to judge a musical act than sportswriters? Well, it worked for me.

Over the years my act morphed from a totally musical act to something I called "The Sports Party" and sometimes "The Boxing Party." These shows include songs about sports and broadcasting. They are also multimedia presentations with video clips of great boxing and sports moments I have announced, trivia questions that give audience members a chance to win prizes, and some lively Q&A interaction between me and the audience. I realized at a certain point that it came down to a choice of having audiences hearing me sing the Great American songbook or having them relive great sports moments, win prizes, and ask questions at an interactive sports/music show. No one had complained about how I handled the songbook, but I rightly decided that choice number two would serve a wider audience. And that is what it has been over these many years. And, besides, if I had stuck with the Great American songbook, it wouldn't have been fair to people like Michael Feinstein, Harry Connick Jr., and Michael Bublé. I mean, with me as competition, how would those poor fellows have ever scratched out a living for themselves?

It's Best Not to Have
Three Beers Just Before You Fight
for the World Title

Remember in chapter 5 when I told you that Bruce "Mouse" Strauss was the funniest boxer of them all? Now that we are here in chapter 11, I'm afraid I have to strip Mouse of that title. Like the WBC I have the power to do this, unlike the WBC there is no exchange of cash involved in this decision. As funny as Mouse could be, I remembered a boxer who was funnier. His name is Tim Tomashek and he earned this "funniest" title while losing a bid for a real one on August 30, 1993.

On that night this journeyman from Green Bay, Wisconsin, did something he never thought possible. He fought for a heavyweight world championship. In the process he created some ESPN folklore, and, like The Mouse before him, ended up guesting on the *David Letterman* show. The events that led up to this were the very definition of improbable.

Our ESPN *Top Rank Boxing* show that night was being beamed out to America from the Kemper Arena in Kansas City. The arena was packed with vocal fans there to see their hero Tommy Morrison defend the WBO title he had won two months earlier from George Foreman. At twenty-four, this grandnephew of screen legend John Wayne seemed destined to do great things in boxing.

He was to defend his title against a marginal contender, Mike

Williams, who was big, tall, and skittish. Williams' unpredictable behavior in the days leading up to the fight had *Top Rank* officials worried that he might pull out of the fight. But not to worry, an hour before our telecast was to begin, Williams was in his dressing room. Oops—fifty-five minutes before our telecast was to begin Williams had left the building, never to return.

Meanwhile, Tim Tomashek was sitting in the stands watching the preliminary bouts with friends. He had just polished off his third beer of the evening when promoter Tony Holden came up and asked if Tim would like to fight Tommy Morrison that evening. Naturally, he said yes.

Tim was about as qualified to fight for a world title as Simon Cowell is to teach a graduate course in diplomacy. He was twenty-eight years old with a record of 35–10, but he had only beaten five fighters with a winning record. Five of his previous six victories before this night came against fighters with *no* wins. Although, reportedly, all of the fighters he beat did have a pulse.

In truth, Tim could fight some. He had gone ten rounds in losing to heavyweight contender Frans Botha and went eight rounds in losing a decision to cruiserweight champ Anaclet Wamba. He threw a lot of punches and had a difficult and awkward style. And, when *Top Rank* found itself just an hour before a national telecast without one of the main event fighters, Tim Tomashek was the very definition of "any port in a storm."

When ESPN officials got wind of the last-minute Williams defection and *Top Rank*'s plan to insert Tomashek into this fight, they were none too happy. Seldom was there a fight for any kind of world title on the ESPN series, and this show was billed as a "Boxing Special." Still, that close to airtime, no one was anxious to pull the plug on the show, so we all soldiered on. Amazingly, *Top Rank* convinced the WBO supervising official on hand to let the fight remain a title match.

ESPN executives were not the only ones dismayed by the turn of events. Add Tommy Morrison's name to the list. Mike Williams already had some credibility issues as a foe for Morrison's first title defense, but Tomashek was even farther down the pecking order. And, Tommy knew Tim personally and said he did not want to fight Tomashek because "He's a nice guy and family friend and he's got that awkward style." He was right on all counts. Tommy grudgingly agreed to go through with the fight.

Tomashek had appeared on ESPN in 1990, so Barry Tompkins and I had some knowledge of his ability and fighting style. We also knew that he was a character in and out of the ring. His nickname was The Doughboy because his pudgy 205-pound frame looked, well, like a doughboy. On this night he looked across the ring at the 226-pound sculpted body of Morrison. If he was nervous about his big moment on boxing's center stage, it didn't show. During the first three rounds of the fight he alternately clowned around and punched. Into the 4th round he had actually thrown almost the exact same number of punches as Morrison—though he landed fewer. Still, he was conducting himself fairly well, and entertaining the crowd with an array of eccentric moves in the ring. At one point he got Morrison in a headlock and gave him what amounted to a "noogie."

In round 4 Tommy finally got his timing to land big shots. He put Tim down, and when Tim got up he battered him for most of the round. After the 4th round the doctor went into Tomashek's corner and asked him, "Do you know where you are?" Tim replied, "Hey Doc, don't you know where we are?" Over Tim's protests, the doctor stopped the fight, and it looked like Tim Tomashek's fifteen minutes of fame was coming to end. Not so, it was really just beginning.

After the fight, I interviewed Morrison and then, with time to fill, we decided to interview Tim, who was still hearing cheers from the crowd for his gallant showing and ever-present smile. Good decision. With an upper-Midwest accent and vocabulary that made him sound like he came right out of the movie *Fargo*, Tim had himself quite an interview. Here's how it went:

AL: We had you on before and you wanted to get on ESPN again, but you didn't expect it would be under these circumstances.

TIM: Oh no, jeepers creepers, not at all . . . everyone at work probably doesn't know I'm on, eh. I work at Shopko. Hi everybody from Green Bay, I love you mom and dad, eh.

AL: This is a big moment for you, and you did perform pretty well for a few rounds. His power was just too much.

TIM: Well, yeah. I'm a good lookin' guy, can't you see. Oh Jesus. He's too strong, eh. He's a very good man, I know all the Morrisons. Just too strong, eh.

AL: You did have your interesting moments in this fight. [During this question a replay of Tim getting Morrison in a headlock and giving him a "noogie" was showing on the screen.] Tell me exactly, from a boxing standpoint, what you were doing here?

TIM: I'm prayin' to mom, mom help me! The guy's so big and so strong, Oh, jeepers.

AL: You got hit by the referee there.

TIM: They're all against me, but I love this crowd, eh. [He waves to the crowd and they cheer him again.]

AL: Well, the crowd loves Tim Tomashek. Why don't you get down and fight in the cruiserweight division?

TIM: I fought the world champion Anaclet Wamba in Europe.

AL: I know; you went the distance with him.

TIM: They tricked me.

AL: How did they trick you?

TIM: Free wine on the flight. Oh Jesus, couldn't pass that up.

AL: Thanks, Tim.

TIM: I love everybody. Hello Green Bay [waves to the crowd and gets another cheer].

I told you he was funny. That interview became an instant classic. And, jeepers, wouldn't you know it, the producers of *David Letterman* came calling for yet another ESPN fighter. He would appear later that week on *Letterman* and charm that late night audience as he had our ESPN viewers.

The *Letterman* fame made him a coveted fighter for Midwest promoters of club fights. His newfound fame, coupled with his wit and personality, made him a big asset to these small shows. Tim went on a tear, winning sixteen of his next eighteen fights, and he beat some ferocious fighters like Winston Burnett who entered the ring with a 20–96–3 mark. Tim won a unanimous decision against him.

Then there was John Basil Jackson, who was to Tim what the Washington Generals were to the Harlem Globetrotters. In December of 1993, Jackson brought his 2–17 record into the ring in Chicago against Tim and left with his eighteenth defeat. Then in April of the following year, Jackson had progressed to 2–28–2, but still Tim was not afraid to face him again, this time in Davenport, Iowa. Again Tim was victorious. It was so compelling they fought for a third time the following month in Omaha, when Tim won yet again. So, these three fights joined the pantheon of great boxing trilogies—Ward-Gatti, Barrera-Morales, Frazier-Ali, and Tomashek-Jackson.

The fun stopped on March 24, 1995, when Tim faced longtime contender Bobby Czyz and was stopped in five rounds. Still, Tim was able to pick up two more wins before retiring from the ring. During his nine-year career, fifty-two foes were vanquished and thousands of laughs were generated by the man they called The Doughboy—the hero of Shopko.

UNDENIABLE TRUTH#12:

List Making Is the American Way

Americans are list makers. In the print and electronic media they make lists that rate things, people, places, events, anything. Americans do that because they like to be judgmental. Americans need winners and losers, thus rankings are essential.

Even though I consider myself to be one-third Canadian, one-third British, and one-third American, the world sees me as an American. So I am obligated to write this chapter in which I make some long awaited lists. As a sportscaster and public figure I hate making lists, primarily because I'm not that interested in being judgmental. (That would the be one-third Canadian coming out in me). Oh, and don't think the Canadian thing is just delusional Canada envy—my mother was born in Canada and came here shortly after her birth. So in a way I do have Canadian ties . . . maybe.

Now the claim that I am somehow one-third British is complete and total nonsense. That is English envy. I have no basis for making that claim. I just want to be British because I love Great Britain and the British people. Is that such a sin? Wait, I do have ties to England. My uncle Stan was from England, but that's by marriage, so I guess that doesn't count. I do feel like somewhat of an honorary Brit, since I joined Channel 5's broadcast team and became the first American commentator ever to do boxing on an English network. Yes, I am reaching here, but please humor me.

Don't get me wrong, I am quite content to be an American—I

love the ideals of the United States and I love the diversity of the national patchwork quilt that makes up our population. So, I love being American—I just want to be Canadian and British too.

Because list making is the American way, it seemed to be the patriotic thing to make a chapter of lists. People are always after me to rank things and make lists. Sometimes people are disappointed that I don't do it. In fact the chief criticism of me as a commentator is that I am too wishy-washy. I live in that gray area. One of my colleagues simply calls me Switzerland. Well, no more. In this chapter I stop my waffling, tear off my cloak of balanced thinking, and let the opinions flow. I will, in fact, be violently subjective. Hide the women and children and let the list making begin!

GREATEST MATCHES I HAVE ANNOUNCED

1. Diego Corrales vs. Jose Luis Castillo I
2. Marvin Hagler vs. Thomas Hearns
3. Israel Vasquez vs. Rafael Marquez III
4. Caveman Lee vs. John LoCicero
5. Juan Manuel Lopez vs. Rogers Mtagwa

I have announced a zillion fights—well, maybe only three-quarters of a zillion, but still, it's a lot. So making this list is hard. The one thing I am sure of is that the 2005 battle on Showtime between Corrales and Castillo is the best of the bunch. I have never seen two men battle with such fierceness and skill. To add to the excitement it created for nine-and-a-half rounds, this match had a dramatic ending. Corrales was knocked down twice in the 10th round, but still managed to come back and stop Castillo in the very same round.

Getting to announce all four of the Vasquez-Marquez fights (the first three were remarkable) on Showtime remains a highlight for me. These two men are both courageous champions in and out of the ring. I hated to see either one lose. Fittingly they ended up splitting the four fights.

The 1981 Lee-LoCicero fight has become a cult classic. The 20 Grand Showroom, a small nightclub in Detroit, was not air-conditioned, and on a very hot and humid July night, the temperature in that room was well above a hundred degrees. How these men could even box in that heat was amazing. This fight makes the list on the strength of the

5th round. In that round LoCicero went down and looked like he was going to lose. He came back and landed something like twenty-five unanswered punches, but Lee would not fall. Still in the 5th round, Lee came back to knock out LoCicero. I still show the video of this amazing round when I do my Boxing Party shows around the country. It never fails to get a huge response. In the fun factoid department: In 1976 LoCicero scored a 1st round knockout over Tony Danza. Yes, Tony Danza the actor was a pro boxer, and the fight with LoCicero was just his second pro fight. Tony posted a respectable 9–3 mark before turning to acting full time.

MOST UNBEATABLE FIGHTERS WHEN AT THEIR BEST

1. Lennox Lewis
2. Muhammad Ali
3. Michael Nunn
4. Pernell Whitaker and Floyd Mayweather Jr.(tie)
5. Rocky Marciano

I know some of you are now contemplating asking for your money back. Lennox Lewis? Yes, Lennox Lewis. I have made radio talks show hosts across the United States crazy with this next statement. In shape, in his prime, Lewis would beat every heavyweight who ever lived. He was too big and he fought tall, and he had power. Yes, I know he lost twice—but he was looking past both those opponents. In a time-traveling big match with greats from the past—I know he would be trained and focused. Here's a question: how many days before the fight should you arrive if you time travel?

I'm sure you are surprised to see Michael Nunn so high on my list. Michael, who was middleweight champion and super middleweight champion in part of the 1980s and '90s, was the perfect boxer in his prime. When he was focused and training with Joe Goossen he seldom lost a round in any fight.

And how, you ask, could I have Rocky fifth when he *never* lost a fight? OK that's a valid point. Wait. I'm thinking of a good response to that. Hmmm . . . Still thinking . . . I have it! My premise is most unbeatable in their prime and at their best. Most of the fighters listed above were undefeated in their prime and at their best. It's just that

The Rock managed to go through his career undefeated, though he had some close calls. See, this is why I hate doing these lists. I just know once this book comes out I will never be allowed in the Italian American Club in Las Vegas again, and I love their pasta.

BEST SPORTSCASTING TEAMS OF ALL TIME

1. Dick Enberg, Al McGuire, and Billy Packer
2. Dick Enberg and Merlin Olsen
3. Tim Ryan and Gil Clancy
4. John Miller and Joe Morgan
5. Joe Garagiola and Tony Kubek

With apologies to the readers in other countries, this list includes only American sportscasting teams, mainly because I don't get to see other teams at work very often. Also, I am the typical linguistically challenged American that only speaks English. So, I would not understand sportscasting teams in many countries. Thus I can't include them. For instance, if I spoke Canadian I would be including a curling announce team.

You can probably see a trend here; I had Dick Enberg in two of the top five teams. Sorry, but if Bob Costas is the perfect studio host (which he is), then Dick is the perfect play-by-play announcer. The trio of Enberg, McGuire, and Packer is the greatest of all time because every role was filled. Dick was the best at his role; McGuire was a genuine character, not the self-created kind we so often see now; and Packer was fantastic at dissecting the strategy of the game.

The two baseball announcing teams on this list demonstrate that you can take different approaches and still be successful. Joe and Tony certainly knew baseball and explained the sport, but they were more jocular and fun loving. John and Joe are purists. Both teams have made baseball enjoyable.

Elsewhere in this book you see more praise of Gil and Tim. Several times on parts of pay-per-view shows I was the third man at the table announcing with them. Though they did nothing to make me feel unwelcome, when I chimed in I felt like someone tapping Fred Astaire on the shoulder to cut in and dance with Ginger Rogers. No sense messing with perfection.

MOST DIFFICULT ATHLETES

1. Jay Buhner
2. Jeremy Williams
3. Mike Tyson

For those of you who are younger and know only the kinder, gentler current version of Mike Tyson, you may wonder how he would even be on this list. Go to YouTube and see the "old" Tyson in action. The miracle is that a guy who used the "F" word to me on national TV (see chapter 2) is as low as third?

Believe me, Jay Buhner, the Seattle Mariners' outfielder, belongs at the top of this list. He got there on the strength of one interview. When I was covering major league baseball for ESPN I spent a fair amount of time covering American League West teams. So, I made a lot of trips to Seattle. On this occasion the M's had just broken out of a horrendous hitting slump to score thirteen runs and get a key win on the last weekend of the season to get them in the playoffs. I was taping an interview with Buhner for *Sportscenter*, and during it I made a very slight reference to the hitting slump and said, "The hitting slump must have been tough for you guys, too bad you couldn't split up those thirteen runs over the last five games." I thought it was a cute comment that might get a funny response. Instead, Buhner unleashed a tirade at the top of his lungs, as we stood in the middle of the locker room. "Why would you even ask about a slump when we just clinched a spot in the playoffs?" He screamed at me for about a minute and a half. The clubhouse, filled with media people and his teammates, went silent as they watched.

I was embarrassed and befuddled. The next question I was going to ask was about his feeling of joy at clinching a playoff spot, but he started yelling at me, so I never got there. He just walked away from me after the tirade, still lambasting me as he went. I had dealt with professional boxers for almost twenty years and few had ever been that rude to me. Shortly after that I was interviewing Alex Rodriguez, and before we started he asked, "What was all that about with Jay?" I didn't have a good answer then, and I still don't. No one has ever accused me of being a hostile interviewer. Mike Wallace I am not.

Jeremy Williams, a fringe heavyweight contender of the 1990s, makes the list because he never liked the questions we asked in our prefight meetings. Much like Mr. Buhner, he was easily offended by certain questions, no matter how benign. At least three or four times per interview he would hear a question and then smirk and say something like, "That's not a very good question." It got to the point that Dave Bontempo and I labeled him "Jeremy the journalist." Finally, during one of the interviews we asked him where he got his journalism degree, since he was so willing to critique our questions.

MOST ICONIC FIGHTERS I HAVE COVERED

1. Oscar De La Hoya
2. Mike Tyson
3. Sugar Ray Leonard
4. Manny Pacquiao
5. Floyd Mayweather Jr.

This list does not include Muhammad Ali because I never covered him on television, though I did cover his fight with Larry Holmes for a boxing magazine. The placement of these men is so tricky, and I know I am wading right into the Pacman vs. Floyd debate that rages in every corner of the Internet and beyond. Some younger fans will be amazed that I could rate Oscar, Tyson, and Sugar Ray above Manny and Floyd. Perhaps it's because in the heydays of those former icons, boxing was less of a niche sport, so they could really transcend boxing. Why is Manny rated slightly above Floyd on the iconic meter? He is more of an international figure. Why is my life on Twitter going to be miserable after this book comes out? Because of the previous statement.

After wading into the water, I'm not sure I am cut out for all this subjective list making. Heck, it's obvious I'm still sensitive about Jay Buhner's outburst ten years ago. I may be a little too thin-skinned to be this opinionated. One time Jim Rome was on my radio show and he said, "Al, you do nice radio. I don't do nice radio. You're supposed to do nice radio—it's what people want from you." So, if you think I've been unfair to one of your favorites in any of my lists, call Jim Rome on the radio and complain; he's better at handling this stuff than me.

Age Is Only a Number, Not a Reality

The thing I remember most about the night of November, 5, 1994, was the noise level. For a moment it actually hurt my ears. A split second after George Foreman's right hand knocked down Michael Moorer, the crowd at the MGM Grand Garden in Las Vegas erupted with the loudest sound I have ever heard in an arena. To say it was deafening is a gross understatement.

That right hand that knocked Moorer out culminated one of the most extraordinary boxing journeys anyone has ever had. It was the night George Foreman became the oldest fighter to ever win the heavyweight title—all this a little over twenty years after he first won the title from Joe Frazier.

I was not in the world of television or boxing in 1973. I was simply a fan watching George shock the world as Howard Cosell repeated his now-iconic line, "Down Goes Frazier." I could scarcely have imagined then that some thirty-nine years later I would call George Foreman a friend, and he would write the foreword for my book. We all get special gifts in our lives—this is a big one for me.

I crossed paths with George during his boxing reincarnation in the 1980s. After a ten-year layoff from the ring, he had returned, at age thirty-eight, intent on winning the heavyweight title again. When he started his improbable comeback against Steve Zouski in 1987, apt comparisons to Don Quixote were being made. This seemed for all the world like a man titling at windmills.

None of us knew that this George Foreman was a different man, one filled with more wisdom, guile, and yes, faith. This is not to suggest that the younger version was not confident or capable. But youth, Fellini-like career circumstances, and Muhammad Ali, all conspired to bring his first boxing chapter to a close quicker than anticipated.

The thirty-eight-year-old Foreman who returned to boxing appeared to be a complete reinvention in virtually every way. I say appeared because the sense of humor that was so prominent in the older George was also present when he was younger. But he showed it less often in his younger years, and the media ignored it when it did surface. They had him pigeonholed as the next Sonny Liston, and humor did not fit into that profile.

George was four fights into his comeback when I first encountered him. He was facing Rocky Sekorski, a club level heavyweight, on our ESPN *Top Rank* series. Along with his promoter *Top Rank*, George had plotted a course that he hoped would lead him back to a world title, and in the process brand him as a unique public personality. The plan was built on fighting often with the most exposure possible. He had started on USA Network and was adding ESPN to the mix for the Sekorski fight. This plan could never have worked unless George was in fact a unique and appealing personality, as well as a resilient and powerful fighter. He was all that.

In 1988 I announced two of George's fights. The first was against Italian heavyweight Guido Trane on ESPN. The Foreman comeback was like gold to ESPN and USA Network because those weekly boxing series got a huge ratings spike when George made an appearance. These two networks chronicled much of this comeback effort and it worked for everyone. George got to work himself back with tune-up fights, and the networks got big ratings.

Every once in a while during the comeback there would be a pay-per-view fight, like his 1988 match with former light heavyweight champ Dwight Muhammad Qawi. As luck would have it, I hosted that show with the great Gil Clancy working as the analyst. Though Qawi was physically overmatched, he helped George create a very exciting fight. Here is where the true appeal of George Foreman as a fighter comes into play. If you look at almost all of George's fights in both phases of his career, there is action. He gets hit, sometimes a lot, and of course he lands punches. Notice I said punches—not just one KO punch that ends things. George threw combinations when he was younger and older. You can make the case that George had as many exciting and entertaining matches as anyone in boxing history.

The match with Qawi was interesting because this much smaller man was finding a way to land some punches. George, who was starting to get his timing back in the eighth fight of his comeback, was landing well also. It seemed a miracle that Qawi was still standing. In the 7th round it ended, and I got to interview George on the telecast afterward. As usual he was funny, glib, insightful, and charming—just what you would expect from a guy who has been getting hit in the head for seven rounds. Right?

The Foreman comeback continued with matches against good fighters, not so good fighters, kind of good fighters, and one or two contenders thrown in there. It was all designed to create enough buzz to get a heavyweight title shot. Remember, when George started his comeback Mike Tyson held the world title. Many thought fighting Tyson would be suicide for George. He always felt he could beat Tyson by fighting him just the way he did Joe Frazier. George would use his height, push Tyson off to break his rhythm, and ultimately land uppercuts and a good right hand that would change the fight.

Over time in his comeback I came to agree. Call me a nut, but I think George would have beaten Tyson. George's chin, even in his later years as a boxer, was as good as any ever in the sport. He was only stopped once, against Ali, and that was from exhaustion and mental fatigue. Ali had taken his will with the rope-a-dope, and George was overconfident thinking he would KO Ali early. I think George would have withstood the punches Tyson may have landed, and he would have physically manhandled him, because Tyson was actually a smallish heavyweight. Bonecrusher Smith was able to go the distance against Tyson doing that, but could not hurt Mike.

And, if George and I needed validation, it would come from Gil Clancy, who had actually trained George in the last fight of his "first" career, when he lost to Jimmy Young by decision. Gil agreed that George had a very good chance of beating Tyson. When we were getting ready to do the Qawi broadcast, Gil explained that you had to land big left hooks to beat Foreman. But a short fighter like Frazier could not get there with that punch. He didn't think Tyson would either. But, he said, if there were a tall fighter with power willing and able to throw powerful left hooks, he might well beat George.

Now we flash forward to 1990 for the "Geezers at Caesars" fight when the forty-one-year-old Foreman took on the thirty-three-year-old Gerry Cooney in Atlantic City. The six-foot-six-inch-tall Cooney had a monstrous left hook, and guess who was in his corner as trainer? Yep, it was Gil Clancy. I remember talking to Gil several times from the training camp, and once he said to me, "Al, I'm telling you, Gerry is going to land some big left hooks, and I just hope Foreman falls. I think he will."

Gil was absolutely right about the left hooks; he was just barely wrong about George falling. In the 1st round of that fight Cooney landed several amazing hooks. He had George wobbled twice, but he did not go down. George has said many times that Cooney hit him harder than any other fighter. George realized that he had to end the fight or he might go. In round 2 he came out with a mission and would stop Gerry with a barrage of punches. I was not involved in covering or calling this fight, and I remember watching this match and dreading the outcome. Gil and George were men I loved and respected, and Gerry was and is also a wonderful guy. I was rooting for a draw, but I knew this fight would end with someone getting knocked out. It turned out to be Gerry.

By the time the Foreman express rolled into the championship depot, it was Evander Holyfield at the station with a title, not Tyson. When George stepped into the ring to fight for the title on April 19, 1991, most boxing pundits and experts still thought George was there only as a novelty, a big name that could create a big-money fight. They doubted he belonged in the ring with the twenty-eight-year-old Holyfield. They were wrong.

Over twelve grueling rounds George took the best Evander could dish out—and it was a lot. He also landed big punches of his own, several times stunning Evander. It was a stirring match that erased all doubts about George as a fighter at his advanced age. I would submit that, even though there was still glory to come, it was this performance, even in a loss, that cemented the Foreman legacy in boxing.

In 1994, after a failed attempt to win the vacant WBO title against Tommy Morrison, there was one last chance for George. Now forty-five years old, he would again have an opportunity to become the oldest man ever to win the heavyweight championship. This time he would face WBC and IBF champ Michael Moorer, who was making his first defense after winning the titles from Evander Holyfield.

The MGM Grand Garden in Las Vegas was filled with boxing fans that were mostly all hoping to see history being made. Except for the few loyal Moorer boosters in the crowd, it was an audience squarely behind George Foreman. I did several interviews with George for ESPN leading up to this fight, and I felt he was very confident. He had been very active in using his celebrity to promote the Morrison fight, and would later say that he had done too much in that area and not paid enough attention to his boxing preparation. For Moorer it was different. He parceled out his "promotional" time. I did an interview with him a few weeks before the fight. After the interview George looked me in the eye. Using a tone of voice as if he were just talking to someone in living room, he said, "Al, I guarantee you I'll win this fight. You can go to the bank on that." I should have gone to the betting window.

So George Foreman, who by the end of the first part of his career seventeen years earlier was almost a punch line, was now a universally loved figure trying to make history. Over the first nine-and-a-half rounds of the match, the MGM crowd was waiting for a chance to cheer. Moorer was dominating the fight, but could not resist the urge to stand and slug with George, and he did get hit with some right hands, but not the perfect right hand.

In round 10 George mixed in one new thing to help set up the right. He landed a left hook to the body that was designed to move Moorer to his left a bit, then he fired a jab and a right hand. That right stopped Moorer in his tracks. The second right sent him down. That was when the eruption of sound enveloped the Grand Garden Arena. When Moorer did not get up, the sound escalated and went unabated for what seemed like minutes.

ESPN had arranged to come to us live, interrupting their programming to do so. Charley Steiner and I had a minute to try and put into words what just happened—we barely scratched the surface. That night's full coverage for *Sportscenter* was something I enjoyed participating in as much as any I did over my years at ESPN. We were covering a story that gave middle-aged men and women all around the globe a feeling that age is just a number, not a reality.

Not lost in all this was the terrible disappointment of Michael Moorer. It had to hurt to be a footnote in history in his first title defense. He had already been living under the shadow of the large public persona of his loquacious trainer Teddy Atlas, and this loss was a devastating blow.

In his foreword to this book George referenced my *Big Fights Boxing Hour* shows, and one of those shows was devoted to his early career. At the end of that show, I delivered these final thoughts:

"Before George Foreman was a personality, he was a puncher. Before George Foreman was a sportscaster, he was a puncher. Before George Foreman was a product pitchman, he was a puncher. Being a puncher is what made all that possible, and as we transport ourselves to his early career, we see that young George Foreman was all about pure unadulterated power. At any age as a boxer, George was capable of giving us knockout thrills."

There is one other thing George is capable of at any age, and that is being a great and loyal friend. I know that firsthand.

If You Think Boxing Isn't a Remarkable Sport, a Trip Across the Pond Will Prove You Wrong

By any historical measure, professional boxing had its true start in Great Britain. You could go all the way back to 1681 and the first bare-knuckles champion James Figg. Or of more recent vintage you could pick 1891 when the National Sporting Club introduced the Marquis of Queensberry rules as part of the sport. I offer this rudimentary history to provide some historical context to this undeniable truth.

I am not one to look for esoteric answers to questions. I like empirical evidence, but sometimes a mixture of the two is where you find the truth. In this case there is ample amount of both to suggest that the sweet science is special in the United Kingdom.

For many years, folks on the United States side of the Atlantic somehow saw boxers from that part of the world as second class. The number of world champions from that area was not overwhelming, and most American boxing fans had never experienced boxing in the United Kingdom. Now the empirical evidence has changed because there have been many more fighters from the United Kingdom who have done well on the world stage, and at a time when boxing in America finds it hard to attract live and enthusiastic crowds, big fights in the United Kingdom do so regularly.

Along with that hard evidence I can add something else that I hope all the "Yanks" reading this book will see through my eyes. When you experience boxing in any of the countries of the United Kingdom, it is a special experience that has an authentic feel to it.

Almost every time I have announced a big fight in Great Britain, Wales, or Northern Ireland, the arena has been packed. That only tells a part of the story. The emotion of the crowd pours down on the ring in a way that is quite different than other places. Two major fights prove this point—these are two fights in which fighters from the United Kingdom pulled off upsets. In both cases they were urged on by crowds that seemed to will them to victory. Both of these fights took place at the M.E.N. Arena in Manchester, England.

The first came on June 4, 2005, when undefeated hometown hero Ricky Hatton challenged Kostya Tszyu for his IBF 140-pound title. I had previously done a Hatton fight for Showtime in the M.E.N. Arena, and I had some idea of the passion that the fans had for Ricky, but it reached a new level for this fight. We were back again to send the match to America on Showtime.

Tszyu was a prohibitive favorite in this fight. He had been a world champ almost continuously for a decade and had a 19–1 record in title fights. Even at age thirty-five he had shown no real signs of decline. The twenty-seven-year-old Hatton was a wildly entertaining fighter and had never lost. But his manic, risk-taking style seemed to make him fodder for Tszyu, a textbook boxer puncher.

Kostya was not a boxer filled with swagger, but he went about his business with a quiet confidence. In our fighter meeting with him the day before the fight, I could feel that he was more than confident. He was *certain* he would win. He didn't shout that out, but it oozed from him naturally. I think he had looked at a video of Hatton and decided, as so many others had, that Ricky lacked the skills to beat him. Hatton and the 17,000 fans that would fill M.E.N. thought otherwise.

The fight was being held well after midnight to accommodate Showtime and the American audience. If the British fans minded, they didn't show it. From the moment Hatton entered the arena to the crowd serenading him with the song "Blue Moon," there was a magic to the evening. I have done thousands of fights, so a hometown crowd being passionate is not enough to sway me. On this night I felt the magic. Going into this match I respected Ricky as a fighter and thought his style had a few more nuances than people acknowledged. Still, I agreed that he deserved his underdog status. At the end of the ring walk I looked at Hatton in the ring and I wrote a note to one of the stage managers that said, "This feels special."

I try and approach every fight without a big preconceived notion about who will win, and I *never* make a public prediction, so it was easy for me to at least let my mind go the possibility that this moment was more than just a crowd getting excited and a fighter looking focused and ready. It did indeed feel like an upset was in the air.

The problem was that all this emotion, I thought, could make Hatton attack in too reckless a fashion and get nailed by Tszyu. I thought wrong. Ricky Hatton harnessed that emotion from the crowd and used it and his will to win judiciously. He fought the smartest and most technically proficient fight of his career that night. He was aggressive, but still mindful of defense. He forced his will on Tszyu throughout the fight, but never lost his head. He made this great champion quit before the last round.

I had been in arenas filled with excitement many times before, but this cathartic win in the wee hours of the morning felt like something different to me. This crowd was channeling the support of a whole city for its native son. It was British boxing at its best.

As a postscript to this, I can say that not every fan in that arena went home happy. Australian movie star Russell Crowe had traveled to the fight to support his friend Kostya Tszyu, who was a resident and fan favorite in Australia. Crowe was at the same hotel as all of us from Showtime, and we found him to be a delightful guy. After the fight we all got back to the hotel very late, maybe 2:30 am. They kept the hotel bar open all night, and Russell and his friends were drowning their sorrows when we got back there. We joined them for drinks, and at about 4:30 am I went up to bed to get about four hours of sleep before leaving for the airport.

When I came down to the lobby four hours later, Russell and his guys were *still* in the bar having cocktails. The next night I turned on the news back in the United States and saw the airwaves filled with the story of Russell Crowe's arrest for allegedly assaulting a hotel clerk with a phone. I noticed in the arrest photos that he had the exact same clothes on as when I had last seen him at the bar in Manchester. Apparently he and his mates had just continued to imbibe until they got on the plane hours later, and then after that on the long trip to New York. So, the weekend did not work out well for either of the famous Australians who made the trek to Manchester.

A little less than a year later I was back in that same arena for another Showtime telecast of the Joe Calzaghe-Jeff Lacy super middleweight title unification match. Calzaghe, the Pride of Wales, came into this fight undefeated and had been WBO champ it seemed since World War II. Well, almost. He had been champion for eight-and-a-half years and defended the crown seventeen times! Lacy, an American, had won his IBF title only two years earlier and defended it three times.

Based on those numbers alone it seems amazing in hindsight that Calzaghe was a fairly substantial underdog in this fight. The media, especially in the States, suggested that he had not faced any tough opposition in those seventeen defenses. This struck me as odd criticism because two of the fighters he defended his title against also fought Lacy for his title. Lacy got them as much older fighters.

I never bought into the cynicism about Joe. We had televised his match 3 years earlier with Byron Mitchell, a hard-punching former champ. Mitchell hit him with the perfect punch and put Calzaghe down in the 1st round. Joe got up and knocked Mitchell out in the second. He showed real grit that night as well as power.

Some of the U.S. press on hand acted as if they were attending a coronation of Lacy as a future superstar. Several boxing Web sites had media polls of who would win, and Lacy garnered well over 90 percent of the votes—mostly from American journalists. I had announced a number of Lacy's fights, including his title win and defenses. I remained skeptical. He had defensive issues, and even in winning fights absorbed punishment. I certainly praised his power and fan-friendly style, but felt compelled to also point out his defensive lapses and lack of hand speed.

I also believed that Jeff suffered from an inflated view of his own ability. He was convinced that he would hit Calzaghe a few times with big bombs, and Joe would fold. Lacy also repeated many times before the fight that Calzaghe threw mostly "slapping punches."

The M.E.N. Arena was filled again. A combination of fans that made the trip from Wales and the local fans all lifted the roof in support of Calzaghe. He performed brilliantly, and all the bravado that Lacy had displayed before the match had dissipated by the 4th round. Calzaghe punished Lacy for twelve rounds. It was as one sided a beating as I have ever seen.

This win brought back memories of Lloyd Honeyghan's 1986 upset over Donald Curry, and Randy Turpin's 1951 win over Sugar Ray Robinson. Both those Brits also upset heavily favored Americans. Calzaghe would further validate his Hall of Fame credentials by beating Mikkel Kessler, Bernard Hopkins, and Roy Jones Jr. and retiring undefeated. If Joe does not make it into the International Boxing Hall of Fame in his first year of eligibility, then an investigation is in order. He's already assured of one vote . . . mine.

While these major fights demonstrate the allure of boxing in the United Kingdom, it's the smaller fights that punctuate that point. When two fighters battle, whether it is for a British title or just bragging rights, the atmosphere is tremendous. The enjoyment level for these fans at a good boxing card rivals anyplace in the world, and exceeds most.

In 2011 one of my "bucket list" items got checked off. I was hired to do boxing on British television. I am proud to be the first American commentator asked to do that. It was even more special because the Channel 5 series, created and promoted by Hennessy Sports, represented the return of the sport to terrestrial television in Britain. This series has also given me a chance to work with Mark Sharman, a man who has helped define British sports television for years as a producer and network executive.

Later in this book I will talk about some of my American announcing colleagues, but this is a good time to point out the excellence of the two men I work with on the Channel 5 telecasts. Mark Pougatch is as good a host as any I have seen, and he was recognized as Sports Broadcaster of the Year in Great Britain. My partner at ringside, Dave Farrar, is superb at calling the fights and brings wit and humor to the job as well. They comprise one of the best announce teams I have ever worked with.

Just before we went on the air for the first time, I said to Mark and Dave, "Well, I better do a good job. If I screw this up there won't be another American asked to do this for another fifty years." It looks like I haven't screwed up too badly so far. At the risk of sounding maudlin,

I can tell you that the warm response I've received from viewers in the United Kingdom has been one of the big thrills of my career.

The posts and tweets have been very supportive, and have also featured some of the wit that the Brits are known for. One fellow posted this on a Web site: "I enjoyed Al Bernstein. A bit of an accent, he needs to work on that." Well, I'm keen on giving it a go. (See, I can speak British!)

I have announced boxing in Cardiff, Manchester, London, and Belfast. In each case the fans and the fighters made an indelible impression on me. Yes, Lord Lonsdale and his National Sporting Club were on to something back in 1891. This boxing thing might stick around for quite a while.

You Know You Are Lucky in Love When Your Wife Faces Potential Death Better Than Most People Face Life

There are two things that can carry us through the worst of times in this fragile thing we call life—humor and purpose. My wife Connie always had both, and in her bleakest of hours, she found even more purpose.

So far in this book I have spared you any ruminating about my personal life. I've done this because my personal life is no more interesting than any of yours, and I'm not narcissistic enough to pretend otherwise. The people and events I've been writing about have more to offer you in the way of intrigue and entertainment. But, for this section of the book, I need to focus a bit on my life, so that I can tell you perhaps the most extraordinary story I've seen in these last thirty years. It just so happens that it involves my wife.

My wife Connie is a funny woman; just ask any of the thousands upon thousands of people she made laugh during a more than thirty-year show business career that started when she was eight years old. Along with her sister Cathy, she made up the Rocco sisters, and they sang and entertained as well as any two women possibly could. Connie also provided comedy in a surprising way. Her often biting humor was wrapped up in a sexy five-foot-eight-inch, 135-pound package that helped her get away with murder on stage. She was a more tasteful version of Chelsea Handler before there was a Chelsea Handler.

As entertainers my wife Connie (left) and her sister Cathy provided enjoyment to many thousands of people. When her performing days ended, Connie played a very different role providing something even more important . . . . hope.

I met her in 1994. So, there she was, beauty, talent, and comic timing . . . what to admire first, I thought. Watching her and Cathy perform night after night I marveled at her ability to constantly adapt to find humor on a nightclub floor or concert stage. She worked without a net, *never* repeating funny lines. It went against all convention. Funny is funny, and if you find funny, you mine it for all it's worth. I've known dozens of comedians, and they all live by that mantra. Connie didn't, and I later realized that this fearless attitude and ability to constantly adapt is a big part of what kept her spirit alive . . . so that *she* could stay alive.

But wait, I'm getting ahead of myself, and I'm probably scaring you with all this foreshadowing about life and death. If this were a movie, the critics would be telling you that this is where the movie, or book, didn't know what it wanted to be. After fourteen undeniable truths filled with ironic humor (wishful thinking on my part), I try to change the tone. Well, I am guilty as charged. And the reason is simple; I could not write this book without telling this story. So, where was I . . . ?

Oh, right, here I was . . . So, after dating for about one year, somehow through sleight of hand, mirrors, cajoling, and every other means at my disposal, I managed to ultimately convince Connie Rocco to marry me. For the first four years of our marriage she traveled around the country performing, I traveled around the country telling people on television why and how men were hitting each other, and about one to two weeks a month we got together to reacquaint ourselves with each other. Life was grand, and it got grander when we had a son named Wes. Connie gave up show business for motherhood, and there were thousands of drunken guys who were now relieved, but somehow sad at the same time, that they would never again feel the sting of her rapier wit. But Connie said Wes gave her a new purpose, and she wanted to enjoy every minute of that purpose.

Mind you, Connie did not stop being funny. She lost all those drunken guys to play off of, but she still had a foil that was even better . . . me. I am a goofball. No really, I am. You may see me as this urbane silver-haired guy in a tuxedo on television, and I hope I am that guy too, but mostly when the TV lights are not on, suave is not my middle name. I lose my car keys five times a day, stub my toe and scream in pain about three times a week, and forget where my car is every single time I park in a parking lot. I break things at an alarming rate and I've turned having household accidents into an art form. Our life is a cross between the Osbournes and the Larry David show, but without the selfishness and profanity of those shows. In the Bernstein household the first undeniable truth of this book applies—There Is Always Time For Humor.

Well, almost always. There weren't many laughs in 2004. That was the year Wes turned four and cancer made a boffo return engagement to my life. It had been such a hit before—taking my dad from me when I was twelve, my mom when I was thirty, and a wonderful brother-in-law from my sister and our family when I was in my twenties. Cancer had a specialty act when playing the Bernstein stage; it made parents disappear so that young children had to grow up without one of the two. In 2004 it was back for an encore.

It started like these stories always start—two hard spots near the underarms, a biopsy, some terrible waiting, and then heartbreak. Most everyone reading this has been touched by a story like this. Its sickening familiarity makes us all cringe. In 2004 Connie Bernstein had stage four breast cancer. The cancer had spread throughout her body, with tumors on her ovaries, liver, back, and pelvis.

I told you we were changing tone in this chapter. Hey—that's more warning than I had. For those lucky ones among you who are neophytes in this cancer stuff, there is no stage five—stage four is as high as cancer gets. So, you can understand given that, and my previous experiences with cancer, how helpless and angry I felt in my private moments.

Of course, this was not about *me*; it was about Connie and a son who looked certain to grow up without one of his parents, a recurring theme in my family. Cancer looked like it was getting ready to bring the curtain down as usual in an abbreviated act three of someone's life. But there were some wild cards in the deck that would take this story in a direction that was surprising in more ways than you might imagine.

First there was my wife's indomitable will, but that card had been played by many people before—some successfully, some not. Still, it was a key factor. Then there was a smart, accomplished oncologist, Dr. Mary Ann Allison, of Comprehensive Cancer Centers of Nevada, who further put to bed this absurd idea that because Las Vegas is, well, Las Vegas, doctors there are not at the top of their craft. And there was the healing arts and nutrition to bolster traditional cancer treatments like chemotherapy that no one with cancer all through their body could possibly do without, even with their inherent dangers to health. A wonderful woman named Pati Kearns brought meditation, Reiki, and other healing arts into Connie's life that bolstered her spiritual strength and centered her mind. And ultimately there was humor, some of it provided by Connie's sister Cathy, who didn't get the laughs on stage in their partnership, but knew how to get them off stage, and did so at just the right moments.

Many of you know what this year-long journey involved. The horrors of cancer are well-chronicled. Connie suffered them all, chemotherapy and its attendant cruelties—nausea, loss of her hair, fear of death every day—but through it all, it was unmistakable that this eclectic combination of efforts to thwart the cancer appeared to be working. It got her in remission five months after being diagnosed with cancer throughout her body.

Then a drug called Herceptin entered the picture. Herceptin, discovered in 1987, is both remarkable and insidious at the same time. This drug is remarkable because for women with HER2+ breast cancer that has spread, it is so effective in stopping cancer in its tracks. That includes 25 percent of the women with metastatic breast cancer. The insidious part of that is there is no drug quite like it yet for the other 75 percent of women in this situation. Connie was one of the lucky ones who could use Herceptin.

Still, even after remission, with stage four cancer, the threat of reoccurrence hangs heavily in the air. And there are plenty of reminders like hair that is slowly growing back after disappearing, the fact that every three weeks (for the rest of her life) Connie has to go in to get an intravenous needle in her arm to take Herceptin, and the constant nerve-wracking tests that could produce despair at any moment.

It was in this environment that we get to the real reason for me interjecting a deeply personal story into this pastiche of a book. Something happened that made it more than just a personal story, something that has universal meaning. Something happened that reminds us that no matter how cynical we might be, we must acknowledge that people with pure thoughts in their heads can change things for other people.

Connie had seen firsthand what hair loss for women had done to their psyche and to hers as well. She wanted to make a difference and decided she would open a hair salon called The Pink Door, which would serve all women, but cater especially to women touched by cancer.

When she told Dr. Allison about this, Mary Ann surprised her with a different idea. Mary Ann had always had the idea that her patients could be helped by having an oasis away from medical treatment centers where they could go to help renew themselves and heal. In Connie she had seen the first complete example of a patient who created her own oasis with healing arts, nutritional help, and emotional support to fight the battle against cancer—and it had worked in a profound way that may well have surprised even Dr. Allison.

She challenged Connie to give up the salon idea and help her make her dream become a reality. Since, to Connie, The Pink Door was about helping people and never about making money, Dr. Allison's vision was one she could embrace fully and even more enthusiastically. They began working on creating a facility that would help all cancer patients, free of charge, with healing arts services, nutritional advice, support groups, and even a library to help patients gain knowledge on cancer-related issues. Here were two women coming together with the will to help others. It was powerful.

The rub here is that Connie was still facing her own mortality, with extensive medical tests every three months and debilitating treatments that still came with the package. Even though she was getting better, it was still not an easy journey. Mary Ann was busy with the mentally, emotionally, and physically exhausting business of trying to save lives. For two women in this situation, building this kind of dream was no easy task.

I marveled at my wife as I watched this professional entertainer somehow find a skill set that allowed her to form and get running a non-profit organization—something so far out of her wheelhouse that she might as well have been promoting boxing matches. (I reached for something as far from non-profit as I could get.) We put together a board of directors from friends, business associates, and others enticed to come along on the journey. They worked hard to make the dream come true that Dr. Allison had envisioned and now Connie had adopted.

We raised money with a twenty-four-hour radiothon, initiated by the ESPN radio affiliate in Las Vegas where I had done a daily sports show for four years. Lotus Broadcasting generously committed twenty-four hours of radio time and many resources to make this event a success. As an annual event it has become one of the most unique events any radio station in the country does for charity. Many of my friends from the worlds of broadcasting and sports have come to help in this crusade. We have now done six of these events, and people like Colin Cowherd, Spencer Tillman, Emanuel Steward, Antonio Tarver, Chuck Liddell, Jim Gray, Jim Lampley, Floyd Mayweather Jr., Bernard Hopkins, Gus Johnson, Forrest Griffin, and many others have come to this event and donated their time and services to be on this twenty-four-hour radio show. I am eternally grateful to all the folks who have helped.

I've been the MC for many events over the years, but serving in that capacity for the annual fundraiser for The Caring Place is by far the most important. This event symbolizes a personal journey that tested my family, but ultimately served to help many others.

As we moved closer to opening this new facility, which would be called The Caring Place, Connie faced another life-threatening challenge. Though her cancer had been in remission due to Herceptin, that drug does not keep cancer from the brain. Perhaps because some residue cancer cells existed there from the time when the cancer had spread, Connie had developed a brain tumor.

My family is hardly the first to go through this kind of continuing ordeal with cancer, and sadly, it is not the last. Still, when you are going through it, you can't think of others who may be feeling this pain—you only know that despair is a daily companion. Despite that, while battling for her life yet again, Connie had still not lost her sense of humor. We had been told that this kind of brain operation could result in thought process changes of some kind—a scary thought to contemplate. When the doctor came out from seeing Connie when she woke up from the surgery, he said, "Your wife is fine. Oh, and she told me to tell you she's now become a Republican." At a moment when I wanted to cry, Connie had again given me a laugh.

Radiation treatments to her head followed, and another one of the many "bonuses" cancer offers—again the loss of all her hair. At this juncture it was almost absurd that Connie was able to continue her efforts to get The Caring Place up and running to help others. Absurd, yes, but also necessary. Through the physical and mental ordeal that she and our family went through, it was this central quest to open The Caring Place that kept her and perhaps me moving forward in life, instead of always thinking of death.

Connie's second ordeal only served to further energize Dr. Allison and the board toward their goal; perhaps subconsciously they felt it needed to be opened while Connie could still be here to see the dream being realized. If that thought was not spoken it hung in the air at every board meeting and every event.

In 2008, The Caring Place opened its doors and began providing free services and programs to anyone touched by cancer and their families. To this day it continues to change people's lives on a daily basis. Thousands of people have come through The Caring Place doors and found help and hope in dealing with their cancer journey in the form of programs, activities, services, and knowledge. To see how remarkable The Caring Place really is, go to its website www.thecaringplacenv.org. You will come away impressed.

There was a feature story about Connie in the *Las Vegas Review Journal* shortly after The Caring Place opened. In it she gave this quote: "A friend once told me that I could live five years with bitterness or one day with happiness. On August third I turn fifty. No one except my doctor thought I would make it. My son is about to turn nine. God, I feel like I'm going to beat the cancer down. I'm here and I'm happy."

Connie not only officiated over The Caring Place's opening as Chair of The Caring Place Board, she remains to this day a healthy and active participant in its efforts to heal the mind, body, and spirit of those touched by cancer. Still, as she will for the rest of her life, every three weeks she gets that IV drip of Herceptin, every four weeks gets two painful shots of Faslodex, she takes a regimen of oral drugs daily, and twice a year she undergoes a battery of tests to make sure there is no active cancer in her body. With all that, every single day she lives life to the fullest—active and upbeat—being a mom, a wife, and an inspiration to all those who learn her story when they visit The Caring Place for help.

Her son, our son, is now twelve years old, and she is still here beating down cancer, not just for herself, but for many others as well.

Connie Bernstein is, after all, a woman who still has purpose and, oh, yes, a sense of humor as well.

Don't Discuss Politics or Religion with Real Cowboys if You Are a Liberal Agnostic

The first thing you need to know is that I admire cowboys, especially real cowboys. They are men who work hard, have a great sense of self, and never use an extraneous word in conversation.

I, of course, am not a real cowboy, but in the last twenty years I've become a reasonably good pretend cowboy. I can ride a horse pretty well, know how to work cattle, and never mistreat my mounts. So, in the western vernacular, I'm not a bad hand . . . especially for a guy who grew up on the south side of Chicago. I never saw any real horses until 1968, and unfortunately those were ridden by the mounted police who were riding herd on me and about five hundred other antiwar demonstrators. Over the last two-and-a-half decades, however, I have had a much more pleasant experience with horses and achieved a modicum of success in fulfilling my cowboy fantasy.

That fantasy was honed in my youth by watching shows like *The Rifleman*, *Wanted Dead Or Alive* and *Have Gun Will Travel*. As a teenager I watched Linda Evans in *The Big Valley* and added another element to my cowboy fantasy, but that's probably a story better left untold.

An example of a great pretend and real cowboy is Ben Johnson. No, I'm not talking about the sprinter who tested positive for steroids.

I'm talking about the movie actor/rodeo star who, to the best of my knowledge, never used performance-enhancing drugs. Ben was not only a world champion rodeo rider, but he was also an Academy Award winner for his performance in *The Last Picture Show*. He appeared in more than two hundred movies and television shows, most of them westerns.

Ben was responsible for me getting to be a pretend cowboy in front of thousands of people. In the late 1980s and early '90s he held the Ben Johnson Celebrity Rodeos, a yearly circuit of rodeos that raised money for charity. I was frequently one of the celebrities participating in these rodeos. They paired celebrities with working cowboys in team roping or team penning competitions.

To quote Billy Crystal in *City Slickers*, I had a roping deficiency. So, I learned how to team pen in order to participate in these rodeos. In team penning you have to cut out three of thirty head of cattle and put those three into a pen. The quickest time wins the competition. You have three riders working together to get this done, and when done properly it is like a ballet on horseback. When it is done poorly (which it sometimes was at celebrity events), it's more like watching Penn Jillette on *Dancing with the Stars*.

This is not the way most of you are accustomed to seeing me. It so happens though, except for handling a microphone at ringside, this is my most natural setting. Over the last 23 years I have logged many hours in the saddle, riding trails, team penning, or just working in the arena to hone my riding skills.

These rodeos attracted celebs like Reba McEntire, Lee Horsley, Richard Roundtree, Patrick Duffy, Doug McClure, James Caan, Larry Mahan, Wilford Brimley, Kay Lenz, Linda Blair, Buck Taylor, and Richard Farnsworth. There were not any sportscasters or Bernsteins participating in these rodeos, so I was something of a novelty. But, since many of the cowboys and folks who gathered at these rodeos were sports fans and, in particular, boxing fans, they were happy to have me and made me feel welcome. If I am good at anything it is assimilating, so I managed not to be a square peg in a round hole.

Still, it was interesting to see the reaction from spectators when my name was announced on the loud speakers and I rode out for the introductions at these rodeos. Many folks had an "I didn't expect to see *you* here!" look on their face. I am sure they were wondering if I would stay on the horse. In fact, I saw several celebrities dumped during the opening ceremonies, even before the competition started.

I was not going to let that happen to me. I was keenly aware that I would be scrutinized more than most of the celebs there that were often cowboy actors and actresses or some other form of western celebrity. So, as I rode my horse on the desert on the outskirts of Las Vegas, I even practiced galloping my horse and waving to simulate those opening ceremonies. If I was going to embarrass myself it was not going to be in the opening moments of my participation. It must have looked pretty weird to people in cars that passed by on a nearby road as they watched me galloping along waving at nobody.

At the first Ben Johnson Rodeo I participated in, a veteran movie actor named Jerry Potter befriended me. When asked by a reporter about me as a rider in the rodeo he said, "He's well mounted." That is a euphemism, for "He's not one of the better team penners around here, but he's riding a great horse." Jerry was being diplomatic—I was pretty green for that first one in 1989, but he was right about my horse. I brought my own horse, Sunset Matt, to the competition, and he was indeed a great mount.

Matt and my current horse Paladin both have been trained by one of the most wonderful women I have ever met, Barbara Callihan. Barbara changed my life as she has so many others by initiating me into the world of horses and riding back in 1988. I had a smattering of horse experience at that time, but she taught me to ride from the basics to the art of team penning. I have known some people who are very good at their craft—sportscasters, performers, television and movie directors and producers, executives of all kinds, you name it. No one does their job any better than Barbara.

As a woman in the man's world of horse competition and training, she fought for every inch of respect and success she garnered, and she has received a considerable amount of both. As a rider she was a champion equestrian, and as a trainer she has sculpted many horses and riders into champions.

Over the years she has worked with riders on every level. The thing that makes Barbara special is that no matter who her clients are, she treats them all the same. If you screw up, she will yell out exactly what you are doing wrong and keep yelling it until you do it right. In the late 1980s and all the 1990s I spent hundreds of hours being drilled by Barbara in the art of riding. She is an unyielding taskmaster, but she is also a nurturing teacher—the best I have ever seen. Heck, she turned a sportscaster into a team penner, what more can you ask?

So, with Barbara's help I sought respect from the cowboy world at the Ben Johnson Rodeos and some occasional appearances at other western rodeos. It was sometimes an uneven journey, like the time I was one of the Grand Marshals of the Parson Rodeo, the oldest rodeo in the United States. The other two Grand Marshals were Ben Johnson himself, and the star of *Gunsmoke* and many other westerns, Buck Taylor. So, among the Grand Marshals I was not exactly the most genuine cowboy in the group. Lumping my name in with those two at a western event is like putting Paris Hilton's name in with a list of Nobel Prize winners.

I managed to look the part reasonably well during most of the weekend's festivities until one embarrassing moment when they were taking the official photo of the three Grand Marshals. For some reason Sunset Matt was crowding Ben's horse and I just couldn't make him stop. It had ruined several photo attempts when Ben just took his boot and kicked Matt in the side—the very same thing I had done a half dozen times. When Ben did it Matt side passed about two feet from Ben's horse, and there he stayed for the photos. Two things struck me about this little incident: The first was that I couldn't figure out what Matt found magical about *Ben* doing it instead of me. Honestly, did he know that this was *Ben Johnson*? The second thing of note was the way Ben managed to do it so casually that it did not in any way put me down.

After this I apologized to him and Buck for making the photo session more difficult, and Ben said simply, "No need pardner, you just keep comin' around and you'll get better and better." I did just that, and at my fourth celebrity rodeo, after I completed my team penning run, Jerry Potter rode up to me and said, "Today you deserve that mount." Ben Johnson was within earshot, smiled and said, "I told you."

Don't get me wrong, I am not suggesting I was ever the best team penner around those rodeos, and I didn't ever win a buckle for first place . . . although I did come close once. In Phoenix my team was within seconds of possibly winning the competition—something depicted in the photo accompanying this chapter. My celebrity teammate somehow got inside the pen and managed to drive all the cattle out of the pen, the *opposite* of what you *want* to do. Not sure what he was thinking at the time. If he had not done that, our time could have been the winning one, and that day would have qualified as perhaps the greatest of my life. OK, maybe the third—my wedding day and the day my son was born would certainly rank higher. As I write this I am months away from getting inducted into the International Boxing Hall of Fame and even that wonderful honor would just barely eclipse winning a buckle at one of the Ben Johnson Rodeos.

So, even with no first-place finishes, I did become a pretty good pretend cowboy. Still, there were moments when I did not assimilate as well as I might have at these rodeos, hence the undeniable truth for this chapter. One time in 1991 at one of the rodeos I was sitting around with some of the "real" cowboys who worked with all of the celebs and tried to make us look good in the arena. These were sturdy men who were maybe just a smidge more conservative in their views than me. Well, maybe more than a smidge.

I had reached a comfort level with them over a period of time and I think I got *too* comfortable. We were talking about where we were all headed after this rodeo ended the next day, and I mentioned that I was going to emcee a campaign event on behalf of Bill Clinton—an event sponsored by a group that advocated seperation of church and state. The room got deathly silent. I had hit the daily double. I was extolling the virtues of a liberal Democrat, and a group that wanted to keep religion and prayer out of government. Oops.

This was close to a moment of glory at one of the Ben Johnson Celebrity Rodeos at which I participated. Sans hat, in the team penning competition, I was trying mightily to keep the cows inside the pen which could have netted my team a great time. There is a rider on the right not seen in this photo who is driving the cows OUT of the pen. That was my fellow celebrity teammate (in name only) who inexplicably scuttled our efforts to get this potential competition winning time. But, I am a Chicago Cubs fan, so I am used to disappointment.

After an uncomfortable silence one fellow asked incredulously, "Why are you doing that?" Sometimes in life I can be, well . . . stupid. Yes that's the word . . . stupid. Instead of doing something to divert the conversation or gloss over this and get back to something more benign, like horses, I explained exactly why I thought Bill Clinton would be such a good president. At that point several of the cowboys took issue with this in fairly blunt terms, and in wrestling with my apparent support of both Clinton and a group that advocated the separation of church and state, they suggested that both Bill Clinton and I were "Godless liberals." I was pretty sure that was not a compliment.

The problem was that I was hard-pressed to give them a rebuttal;

the proverbial shoe fit pretty well. So, instead I launched into a little speech about all the freedoms our country allows and that it's the differences that make us stronger as a nation, etc. I even suggested that they themselves represented that idea because they were self-reliant men who worked hard and well alongside others, but still embraced the idea of personal freedom above most everything else.

Things had gotten pretty heated at one point and I was hoping that my little speech had hit home. I'd hoped that for two reasons: First, I did not want all these guys hating me, because I liked and admired them so much. Second, I did not want any of them punching me. At that moment, the man who had ridden on my team that day in team penning put down his beer, came over to me, and slapped me on the back. He said, "Well, hell, for a Commie pinko, you're still not a bad guy. Let's have another beer." The room erupted in laughter, and everyone did indeed have another beer.

My little speech, designed for self-preservation, was totally sincere. My admiration for cowboys (and cowgirls for that matter) and the virtues they represent knows no bounds. In fact, lack of boundaries is what the horse and western experience is still all about. When you are riding a beautiful trail in open country, you have stopped time while you connect with the land you are covering and the horse you are riding, and anyone who is riding with you. The boundaries of time and space are erased. That kind of experience transcends personal boundaries as well, and so does working together to chase some cows into a pen. If you are a decent hand, and you treat your horse and fellow riders with respect, you can even get away with being a Godless Liberal. But, it's still best to keep that last part to yourself.

Sometimes the Good Old Days Really Are the Good Old Days

As decades go it's pretty hard to top the 1980s. In boxing it was a time of great fights and great fighters. In sports television it was a time of terrific programming and unbridled decadence and fun.

About a week before the September 16, 1981, megafight between Sugar Ray Leonard and Tommy Hearns, I had breakfast with the great Gil Clancy. For me it was like dining with boxing royalty. I was only a year or so into my boxing broadcasting career and Gil was already a surefire Hall of Famer who had done everything in boxing. He trained and managed world champions, served as matchmaker at Madison Square Garden, and became the best ringside analyst ever on television. The only man who rivals him today is another Hall of Famer Emanuel Steward, who has had a similar career path. I have learned about boxing from both men, and I value the friendship I shared with Gil, and still share with Emanuel. They are both special men.

At one point in the breakfast Gil made a profound statement of what was to come. "You know," he said, "I've seen some amazing things in boxing, but I think what we are going to see from this group of fighters will rank with the best. It's going to be special."

We all know that Gil was so right about the boxing we would see from "this group of fighters" in the '80s. The group he meant was Marvin Hagler, Sugar Ray Leonard, Roberto Duran, and Tommy Hearns. They were dubbed the Four Kings in an excellent book by the late George Kimball.

They were not the only great fighters of the decade. You can add names like Alexis Argüello, Aaron Pryor, Larry Holmes, Salvador Sanchez, Evander Holyfield, Wilfredo Gomez, Michael Spinks, Julio Cesar Chavez, Mike Tyson, and Azumah Nelson. However, the Four Kings were the focal point of the decade, even among these other giants in the sport. That makes it even more amazing.

I could not have imagined at that 1981 breakfast that I would join Gil and Tim Ryan as the most often heard voices chronicling the exploits of the Four Kings in the 1980s. I would end up on the pay-per-view telecast of these fights:

> Hagler vs. Duran—1983
> Hagler vs. Juan Domingo Roldan—1984
> Hagler vs. Hearns—1905
> Hagler vs. John Mugabi—1986
> Hearns vs. Iran Barkley—1988
> Duran vs. Barkley—1989
> Leonard vs. Duran III—1989

All but one of those fights were in Las Vegas, where most of the drama surrounding these four fighters was acted out. Caesars Palace and the Las Vegas Hilton were the two casinos that hosted major fights. The excitement surrounding these big fights was palpable, and it was especially electric for the Marvin Hagler-Tommy Hearns fight in 1985.

The night before the fight, I sat in the Olympic Lounge at Caesars Palace and drank in the atmosphere. One of the many celebrities out that night was Rodney Dangerfield, and that was the first night I met him. He came up and introduced himself and we had a drink together. As you read in chapter 10, just two years later Rodney would be sitting in the audience in that very lounge listening to me sing. Music was not discussed that night. It was all about the great fight we expected to see the next night.

This telecast had significance to me because I was doing it with ABC announcer Al Michaels. ABC had requested that the promoters, *Top Rank Boxing*, put Al on this show so they could see how he and I worked together. I was under consideration to be Al's partner when he started doing the ABC boxing broadcasts. So, this was heady stuff for me. To add to it, broadcasting legend Curt Gowdy was hosting our telecast.

It was a beautiful April night for this fight, and the Caesars Palace outdoor arena was full. I remember a feeling that I had as Tommy Hearns started his walk into the arena and the noise level started to swell—a feeling that I have consciously duplicated every time I can. I had a few moments to just let the moment sink in, and I thought about how there is no place I would have rather been than at that broadcast table on that night. Now I have a ritual at every fight I ever do. At some point before the main event when I have a moment to reflect, I think the same thoughts. It started in 1985.

And boy was I right about being lucky to be there. We know what transpired over the two-and-a-half rounds that fight lasted. In the opening moments when Tommy landed that huge right hand, it set in motion some of the best moments in middleweight title history. Marvin has said many times that that right hand was as hard as he had ever been hit. He attacked like a maniac and Hearns responded in kind. The 1st round was astonishing.

Al Michaels had been pretty passive in his announcing during the undercard, not really that engaged. In that 1st round of the main event he came alive. Hell, you'd have to be dead not to come alive for that round. By round 3 Marvin had terrible cuts that looked like they would stop the fight at any minute. It was simply a race against time. Would Hearns go down before he could get the fight stopped on cuts?

Tommy never had his legs under him in that fight. Had he been able to box more, as he did against Leonard four years earlier, he might have won that fight with a TKO due to the cuts on Hagler's face. Marvin refused to let that happen.

I didn't receive a call from ABC after that show. It turned out an ABC boxing producer/executive, Alex Wallau, decided *he* wanted to be the analyst on the ABC boxing shows. And he got it. I didn't see that one coming. I figured if I lost out it would be to an actual sportscaster. Go figure.

I didn't lose any sleep over it; I was having too much fun. In fact, sleep was one thing we did not do very much of during those big fight weekends in Las Vegas. The "less is more" bromide was lost on me and my media and boxing compatriots when it came to having a good time. I remember a night one of our group hosted a dinner party at the Palace Court Restaurant. You could actually get neck massages from lovely ladies while you dined there. The food was gourmet and the atmosphere was pure luxury. This dinner party featured twelve guests. On that night more than twenty bottles of Cristal Champagne were consumed, every "masseuse" had a career night at our table, and the appetizers alone could have fed a family of four for a month. At the end of the evening the bill approached $15,000. And, mind you, that was in 1987!

We all worked hard during fight week, but when we were not working you would find us at the Caesars Palace pool, where we always had cabanas reserved. If it were possible to actually build a little condo at the pool, we would have done so and lived there.

The only major fight involving one of the Four Kings that was not in Las Vegas provided an atmosphere very different than what I just described. On February 24, 1989, the Atlantic City Convention Center would play host to the Roberto Duran-Iran Barkley fight. On the day of the fight one of the worst blizzards in years swept across the East Coast. Layers of snow and high winds shut everything down. We wondered if anyone would even show up to see the fight.

It was a special night for me because I would be working on the telecast with none other than Gil Clancy. My good friend and then only occasional collaborator, David Dinkins Jr., was the producer, and Bob Dunphy was the director. I was with the A team. These men, along with Tim Ryan, had raised the bar in network coverage of boxing. I didn't often have a chance back then to work with a group like this.

As we televised the under card an amazing thing was happening. We saw people coming in on a steady basis until they filled the Convention Center. Somehow these fans had made it there.

Barkley was making the first defense of the middleweight title he had won earlier that year in a huge upset over Tommy Hearns. Duran was a big underdog in this fight, and David Dinkins remembers the prelude to this fight. "This was yet another fight where it looked like Duran had finally run his course, especially at middleweight. He was facing a fighter in his prime a weight class too big for him." He added, "This was supposed to be Barkley's chance to finally break through and achieve stardom."

The weather outside was frightful, but inside it was pure boxing bliss. These two men produced a classic battle. The fight looked like it was going to form early with Barkley outpunching and outboxing Duran. Then Gil showed his savant side and started giving the viewers foreshadowing of a Duran comeback. As always, he was right. Duran turned it up and was right back in the fight. Ironically I thought Barkley fought one of the best fights of his career, but Duran found magic that night. He would put Barkley down in the 11th round and closed strongly. At the end of the fight, as if more drama were needed, the microphone for ring announcer Michael Buffer did not work. He had to yell out the scores . . . Duran won a split decision. I still believe Iran won the decision as one of the judges said, but it was certainly no robbery.

David summed up the evening very well, "Duran went to that special reserve to do it one more time. If you were great once, you can still be great again for one more game or one more fight. The great ones know their way there for that moment."

I have watched that fight maybe ten times on YouTube and I never tire of it. It is probably the best night of my more than thirty years of broadcasting. The boxing was superb, amazing drama unfolded in front of us, and it was one of the best live television shows I have been involved with. It is certainly the best-announced fight I have ever been a part of doing. Gil was beyond remarkable, and perhaps some of his pixie dust rubbed off on me. I think it was my best performance as a play-by-play announcer.

After this win, Duran would participate in the last major fight of the 1980s, a December 7, 1989, date with Sugar Ray Leonard. Mirage played host to this fight and on this night the outdoor venue posed some problems. The desert winds had kicked up during the day and there was even some concern about holding the fight. I would not be calling this fight, but would be serving as co-host along with Los Angeles—based sportscaster Jim Hill. We were located up in a perch overlooking the ring. This makeshift tower seemed sturdy enough until the winds came. We were rehearsing in the late afternoon, and all of a sudden Jim and I felt like we were swaying. There was a very good reason for that—we *were* swaying. The winds had reached thirty-five miles per hour gusts, and our little tower was going back and forth. Inside the TV production truck they wanted us to continue rehearsing. "Just a few more minutes," we heard through our earpieces. Jim and I looked at each other and agreed without speaking it was time to go. We politely excused ourselves because we had this crazy fear of dying. Silly, huh? I was happy about our decision when we were on the ground watching this little tower sway in the wind. They found us a new location—a safer one.

For all the great moments of the 1980s, the decade went out like a lamb not a lion. This third match between Leonard and Duran was a dull affair. Ray boxed effectively and Duran looked like he was walking in mud. It was really the only match between the Four Kings that was lackluster. You knew this was the end of this remarkable run of fights featuring these four extraordinary men.

Gil had called the action at ringside with Tim. Afterward I reminded Gil how prophetic he was at that breakfast we had back in 1981. I asked him whether this run of fights was indeed the most special thing he had seen in boxing. He said simply, "And then some." Amen.

People Who Make Us Laugh Really Like Boxing, and Who Knew the King of Comedy Is a Bit of an Expert?

I have known many comedians, and almost to a person they are big boxing fans. Maybe it's because, like boxers, they suffer for their art.

I have interviewed so many comedians on the radio, and they love to talk boxing. The list includes Jackie Mason, David Brenner, Jay Mohr, Alan King, Damon Wayans, Pat Cooper, Steve Rossi and Marty Allen, Jason Sudeikis, and many more.

Jay Mohr launched into a pitch-perfect Larry Merchant impression while on the show, creating his own version of Larry calling the George Foreman knockout of Michael Moorer. He then added Harold Letterman to the mix to create an on-the-spot hilarious routine.

During her singing career my wife Connie and her sister Cathy performed with many comedians. Early in our marriage they were opening at Resorts International for Don Rickles. After they left the stage, Don made his entrance to perform and looked down at me and said, "We have one of the great sportscasters here tonight. Please welcome Mr. Al Bernstein. Al is married to one of those two beautiful Italian girls you just saw—the Rocco Sisters. Al and Connie just got married. Al, I'm sure you two will be very happy . . . until she finds out you're a Jew. No, I'm kidding, I think she already knows. You got maybe three weeks. I love Al announcing the boxing matches. He knows everything. He's calling the matches telling us this guy beat Gonzales and the other guy fought Sanchez and then before that he lost to Johnson. He thinks we care. Al, we don't even know who these guys are. You're the only one that knows." For a four-night engagement I sat ringside to hear my wife sing, and every night Don beat me up to the delight of the crowd.

Jackie Mason enjoyed giving me a hard time when he guested on my show. "Al, to be honest with you, when I hear you on TV I have no idea what you're talking about. It makes no sense at all. Who did you sleep with to get that job . . . what's his name? I never heard anything like it. I can't believe you're still on television." He did three minutes like that, and I was wiping tears away.

Garry Shandling is a huge boxing fan and he is co-owner of a boxing gym in Los Angeles. I met him on Twitter. In that medium he is very funny as well. Actually, they have not invented a medium in which Garry wouldn't be funny.

About five years ago I read a book called *Dean and Me*. In it the great Jerry Lewis recounted the history-making ten-year partnership he had with Dean Martin. It was a partnership that changed show business and made both men transcendent stars. The book was funny, touching, unflinching, and wildly entertaining. I am a devotee of show-business memoirs. This book is the best of the genre.

I was so moved by its honesty and wit that I had to try and communicate with Jerry Lewis, even though I had never met him. I knew we did have a mutual friend in Las Vegas and I asked her if she could possibly pass along a note for me. She said she would deliver my note, and I hoped he would look at it to know how much I admired what he did in the book.

About two weeks later I was out having dinner and checked my phone messages, and I heard in a very distinctive voice, "Hi, this is Jerry Lewis. I got your lovely note and I am kvelling [a Yiddish word for being proud]. To receive that from you was wonderful." Even though I had just written a note to him and I did have every expectation he would get it, I *still* didn't quite believe I had received a phone call from Jerry Lewis.

I was reminded of a story Michael Buffer told. One night his phone rang and when he answered he was also greeted by a very distinctive voice that said, "Hello, Michael. This is Cary Grant. I was watching you the other night and I loved the tie you were wearing, I wanted to see where you got it." Michael assumed it was someone pulling his leg, but it was not. Michael said it took a while for Cary to convince him he was really Cary Grant.

I was pretty sure this really was Jerry Lewis. There are icons in this world, and then there are icons. Then there is a category just above that, and that is where you will find Jerry. Only a handful of people reside at that address. To my great joy Jerry has become a friend of mine. During this friendship I have learned that there is something Jerry knows almost as much about as comedy—that would be boxing.

I found out that Jerry is not only a big boxing fan, but he also has a rich history with the sport. And, he has a great feel for the sport. Sometimes that feel has been a little too hard. He and Dean were very good friends with Rocky Marciano. One night Rocky came to see them and was standing in the wings with Jerry as Dean finished a song. When Dean finished and Jerry started to go out to the stage Rocky said, "Do a good show," and gave Jerry an affectionate "love tap" on the chin. Jerry remembers that moment, "I walked out to my partner on stage in front of six thousand people, and Dean said to me, "What the hell happened to you? I was swiveling. Rocky didn't mean to hit me that hard, but he did. He thought I was making believe as I went on stage. I wasn't making believe."

Jerry was also friends with Sugar Ray Robinson. "Ray was prolific in his thoughts. He was a bright man and he was bright inside the ring. He had the game where he could say at the end of the chess game—check. He had it all."

Jerry has some interesting ideas on the sport, and one is his refusal to ever bet on a boxing match. "I can't bet on boxing. It makes me feel tacky. I don't want to bet on a person who is going to hurt another person. It becomes different when there is money involved," he said. I thought about that statement afterward and I realized he's right. Rooting for someone in this kind of sport *is* different than betting on him.

I was in Jerry's office talking with him about a month or two before the Shane Mosley-Manny Pacquiao fight, which we were going to do on Showtime. I suggested that while Mosley should be the underdog, he would make the fight interesting at some point, like he did briefly when he hurt Floyd Mayweather Jr. Jerry shook his head and said, "This will not be a competitive fight. Manny has too much for him, he's in another league. It will go twelve, but Manny will dominate him." So, I guess you know which one of us was right.

Jerry once said to me, "We've lost so many pertinent people to the sport. I always wish Bert Sugar should live a thousand years. It's like looking at a Jewish Encyclopedia—if you want to know something about boxing you get to Bert Sugar." I thought about that comment when Bert passed away. Hard to imagine the sport and this world without Bert.

When I talk to Jerry, I constantly have to remind myself that he has known *everyone*. I mean, who else can say they hosted shows over the years with the likes of Al Jolson and Muhammad Ali as guests? When he tells me stories about knowing The Rock or Sugar Ray or Joe Louis, it feels like I'm in a time traveling machine. Then when he gives me good analysis of a Showtime fight I have just announced, I know the man I'm talking to is very much in the present.

If it is in every comedian's DNA to be a boxing fan, then it should not be that surprising that the king of comedy is such a big fan. And he is more than a bit of an expert. Thankfully he has no designs on my job . . . I hope.

Formal Wear
Can Upgrade Appearance,
but Not Content

Back in 1891, the National Sporting Club in England started holding professional prize fights at their club. As you read elsewhere in this book, it was the introduction of the Marquis of Queensberry rules into the sport, and really the birth of professional boxing as we know it today. These shows were groundbreaking and special and they wanted to further accentuate that, so the club made formal wear mandatory for all who attended. Since the membership was mostly the upper crust of English society, this was not a big imposition. Most members had formal wear hanging somewhere in the closet.

This started the tradition of ring announcers and then sportscasters wearing formal wear on special boxing occasions. The big fights I worked on in the 1980s all called for tuxedoes. At age thirty-two I owned zero tuxedos. At age thirty-nine I owned eight. I had more tuxedos than sport coats. Something about that seems unnatural.

These big fights that I have talked about elsewhere in this book were, by any definition, extremely significant. Wearing formal wear for those telecasts was certainly appropriate. One or possibly two tuxedos would have sufficed for those events. But, in the late 1980s and early 1990s, my announcing partner Barry Tompkins and I wore tuxedoes forty-five to fifty times a year doing the *Top Rank Boxing* series on ESPN. Why? Only Steve Bornstein knows the answer to that.

Bornstein had moved up the ladder at ESPN to become president and CEO. Some would advance the theory that Steve might be living, breathing proof that the Peter Principle is wrong. You can be promoted past your level of competence. Does the term "Emperor with no clothes" ring a bell?

Bornstein passed an edict that we would wear tuxedos for the *Top Rank* series. This struck us as odd because a main event of Terrance Ali vs. Martin Quiroz, though fun and competitive, didn't quite have the magnitude of Sugar Ray Leonard vs. Roberto Duran. I guess Steve thought that by putting the announcers in formal wear it somehow made our fights major boxing events. This is the same as putting a fancy title like Network President in front of someone's name and expecting that to make the person a better fit for his job.

Before anyone misinterprets my remarks about the *Top Rank Boxing* series, I want to tell you that I believe that series was one of the greatest achievements ever in the sport of boxing. For almost eighteen years Bob Arum and his Top Rank Company came up with close to fifty cards a year for a national network. No one else has ever done that in the history of television and boxing. I actually think that by putting us in tuxedos Bornstein showed that he didn't grasp the true appeal and genius of the series. This was boxing's version of Triple-A baseball, really good and interesting and the stepping-stone to the next level. Perhaps Steve felt guilty about not buying other, more-important matches for ESPN to televise, and so he wanted to dress these up to be something different.

In other chapters you can sense my affection for the *Top Rank* series. If Bob Arum and *Top Rank* had never created that series, I am not sure I would have had a thirty-year sportscasting career, or be writing this book right now. The series featured dozens of future champions on the way up, many classic slugfests, and enough crazy moments to fill a book. Actually they've helped fill this one, haven't they?

Wearing a tuxedo almost fifty weeks out of the year presents a fashion challenge—that's how I ended up with eight tuxedoes. That's not the big problem. In the movie *Steel Magnolias*, one of the characters says, "The difference between man and animal is man knows how to accessorize." When you have to accessorize formal wear fifty weeks out of the year, it's not easy. You need vests, ties, cummerbunds, shirts, etc. At one point I even had string ties that I wore with my western tux.

Both Barry and I were desperate men, and desperation can lead to strange things. On one show Barry did not have a tie with him, and I loaned him what was one of my favorites. It was a great silver and black bow tie. About six months later I actually complimented him on how nice his tie looked, and he said, "You know, actually I think this one might be yours." It was the one I loaned him. I said, "It looks better on you, maybe you should keep it." So, the need to accessorize had turned Barry Tompkins, an honorable and honest man, into an inadvertent tie thief. It got to the point that I couldn't stop buying tux accessories. I was addicted. And there is no Tuxedos Anonymous.

There was one place on ESPN where wearing formal wear was in order. I often wore a tuxedo on our *Sportscenter* coverage of big fights involving the likes of Oscar De La Hoya, Mike Tyson, Evander Holyfield, Lennox Lewis, and Roy Jones Jr. Back then ESPN would send an army of people out to cover these big fights. It included talented and delightful producers like David Brofsky, Barry Sacks, Craig Mortali,

For almost seven years I wore a tuxedo nearly every week of the year on the ESPN Top Rank Boxing Series. Broadcasting challenges became secondary to the main problem, how to accessorize week after week. In this photo from the early days I still sported the basic look. But soon I knew I had to change it up on a regular basis. Why did I face this agonizing dilemma? Only a misguided network executive knew the answer, and he wasn't telling.

and Tim Hayes. Most often joining me on camera was Charley Steiner. We also frequently had *USA Today* columnist Jon Saraceno joining our announce team.

Back then CNN had an active sports department, and there was a competition between CNN and ESPN to see who could get information about these fights on the air first. Rudy Martzke, the sports-television writer for *USA Today* would note in his column the time of first coverage and who got the first interview. Nick Charles, who would later be my colleague at Showtime, often did the interviews for CNN, and usually I did them for ESPN. Despite the nonsense in Rudy's column and the pressure from our respective networks, Nick and I vowed we would not battle each other for the first interview. We simply alternated who went first from one big fight to another. That's not an arrangement you can make with everyone, but Nick was a true gentleman. His death in 2011 left a huge hole in all our hearts and in sports television.

Doing the *Sportscenter* coverage provided spontaneous moments that are hard to reproduce. One of the best for me came after Riddick Bowe's victory over Evander Holyfield in their third fight. I was interviewing Holyfield, and Bowe showed up unannounced and joined our interview. I simply facilitated a conversation between the two men for several minutes, interjecting only when necessary. Two gallant warriors sharing honest thoughts with each other after a slugfest. It was the best postfight coverage interview I have ever been associated with.

By 2000 ESPN had ramped down its *Sportscenter* coverage of big boxing matches, but they ramped it up again for the 2002 battle between Lennox Lewis and Mike Tyson. Of all the fights I covered for *Sportscenter* over a span of fifteen years, this one was the only one in which I was absolutely sure I knew who would win. I never felt Tyson had any real chance of winning this fight. I didn't like making prefight predictions when we covered for *Sportscenter*, but by 2002 ESPN was in the "opinion is king" mode, so I had to give a prediction. I said flatly, "This is not a competitive fight. Mike Tyson cannot win." I seldom put things in such stark terms. Even I was surprised to hear that come out of my mouth that way when I responded to Brian Kenny's question. On this night I was right—Tyson was demolished by Lewis.

The coverage of this match was also notable because it featured Jeremy Schaap in one of his stints in boxing coverage as an interviewer and feature reporter. There are some fine journalists working at ESPN, but Jeremy and Bob Ley are by far the best. Jeremy and I were both appalled at Tyson's boorish prefight behavior (nothing new for him). Among his transgressions was attacking Lewis at a prefight press conference. Jeremy's viewpoint on Tyson's behavior did not affect the way Jeremy handled the more docile postfight Tyson during a bizarre self-denigrating interview. It would have been easy for Jeremy to pile on a bit, but instead he gently guided Tyson through this as if he were his analyst. It produced mesmerizing television.

This was the last of the big fights I covered at ESPN. I left for Showtime in 2003. The tales of covering all those big fights are spotted throughout this book. My colleagues and the great stories we covered made them all memorable experiences . . . even the ones in which I did not wear a tuxedo.

When the Lights Go Out
Anything Can Happen

"If you spend an evening you'll want to stay
Watching the moonlight on Cape Cod Bay
You're sure to fall in love
With Old Cape Cod"

Before I visited Cape Cod, Massachusetts, for the first time in 1983, I had heard those song lyrics sung many times by the likes of Frank Sinatra, Jack Jones, and even Bette Midler. What a delightful picture it painted for me. My reality did not quite match up to that.

The ESPN *Top Rank Boxing* series rolled into Cape Cod for an August 11, 1983, middleweight fight between local hero Sean Mannion and New York's Danny Chapman. Mannion had just beaten undefeated contender In-Chul Baek, and he was poised for a world title shot. The twenty-two-year-old Chapman was a tough journeyman with an 11–8 record. This was the quintessential tune-up fight.

The match was going mostly according to form, but Chapman was starting to come on as the ten round fight headed toward the finish line. In the 9th round Chapman looked like he hurt Mannion. In the 10th round he *definitely* hurt him. Just at the moment when things were getting a bit perilous for Mannion, the entire arena went dark. There was a total blackout. It was a little hazardous for everyone for a few minutes. The alcohol had flowed freely all night and the crowd was, shall we say, a colorful lot. Miraculously, in about five minutes the lights came back on, and when they did there were fistfights in progress and the atmosphere in the arena was charged, to say the least. A few items were then hurled at the ring just for good measure.

Interestingly, the lights came back on almost immediately following the ring official's ruling that the fight would not continue—a pretty good development for the hometown fighter. Chapman's manager/trainer Bob Miller smelled a rat. The timing of the blackout was, well, let's say too perfect. The conflicting answers about the blackout suggested that it might have been caused by ingenuity, not electrical failure. Wouldn't you know, we found out days later that there was no power outage reported in that area that night, so somehow the lights had gone out *only* in the arena. Curious.

Mannion got a decision win even with the shortened final round. Two fights later he would get his title shot, but lose a decision to Mike McCallum. For Chapman, this missed opportunity sent his career into permanent "opponent" mode. He would lose seventeen of his last twenty fights.

So this fits in with some strange situations in the early years of the *Top Rank* ESPN series. The surrealism of this one was not done for me when I signed off the air. After the show I had to go to the bathroom, having gone through a two-and-a-half-hour show on the air without a break. As I was standing at the urinal a man dressed completely in black leather came in and stood at the urinal right next to me, even though others were available. Before unzipping to urinate, he reached in his back pocket and took out a very big handgun and placed it on the urinal.

I was wide-eyed at that point, wishing very much that I had concluded my business, but alas I had not. He looked at me and said, "What do you think about the fight?" I looked down at the gun, thought for a moment, then looked at him and said, "What would you like me to think?" He just chuckled and didn't say a word. A few moments later we were both ready to leave. As he was putting the very big gun inside the back of his pants, he turned and said to me, "Be careful. A lot of people were drinking tonight. You might run into somebody who's crazy." Well, well, a little too late for that warning.

I did not fall in love with Cape Cod Bay.

Breaking Down the Fourth Wall
Can Be Dangerous

Being on television allows you a certain detachment from the public you serve. Some people who work in front of the camera on television love that detachment. They don't feel the desire or the need to reach beyond that to interact with people. I am not one of those people. I love interacting with the folks who I know are already getting dialogue from me on television. I enjoy getting some back from them.

In the theater they refer to an invisible "fourth wall." On stage, if you get out of character and talk directly to the audience you have broken the fourth wall. A friend of mine said to me recently, "You like breaking the fourth wall, don't you?"

I do.

Some of my television brethren invent ways not to do it. I invent ways to smash through that fourth wall. Maybe that's why I like Twitter so much (more about that in chapter 28). That interaction is immediate. A creative and patient man named Dan Parks, president of Corporate Planners Unlimited, Inc., has been my shepherd through the social media, creating my presence on Facebook, Twitter, Google Plus, and other social media locations. When I started this journey those things were as foreign to me as ethics and loyalty are to most college football and basketball coaches. Now, however, I am a fully functional social media participant, using these new tools to break through the fourth wall on a daily basis.

One of the less high-tech ways in which I have interacted with sports fans is through my live appearances. Al Bernstein Live, a company superbly run by Adie Zuckerman, sends me out across the hinterlands to break the fourth wall. Through that company I am booked to do my Boxing Party stage show, give after-dinner speeches, appear on panels, etc. Adie, who also happens to be my sister, is more than qualified to protect me from the pitfalls of business, but she can't protect me from the crazy things that happen on the road at my extemporaneous and interactive Boxing Party shows.

I do the show at casinos and often theaters around the country. As I explained in chapter 10, I morphed my nightclub act into this some years ago. The show includes my sports music, trivia questions for audience members to win prizes, and funny and action-packed video clips. In addition to the trivia there is audience interaction in a question and answer period in which people can ask me any question they want. Sometimes my answers don't quite work.

At one show in the 1990s, up in Great Falls, Montana, I did a Boxing Party show that was also a tribute to Todd Foster, who was an Olympic boxer and a lightweight contender from that city. He is a true hero in Montana and a wonderful guy. During the Q&A someone asked me who would win if Rocky Marciano faced Mike Tyson. Unfortunately I said Tyson. That was a mistake. I don't know if it is wrong, since Stephen Hawking has not yet figured out time travel we don't know. In any case it was not correct because about 90 percent of that audience disagreed with me . . . a lot.

We were having a grand time up to that moment. They loved my sports songs and the video clips of great and funny boxing moments, and I had given away a lot of prizes in return for people answering trivia questions. We were all one big happy family, until I answered that dreaded Marciano-Tyson question. I was being berated from all sides, and the more I joked and the more I tried to change the subject, the more they concentrated on that. One older gent got up and said, "I was at the fight when Rocky beat Jersey Joe Wolcott. He is the greatest fighter of all time. You, young man, you need to know that." He received a huge ovation. The previous biggest ovation of the show had been when I sang a musical tribute to Todd Foster. So, now I knew I was in trouble.

I walked down the middle aisle of the crowd, and when I got halfway I said, "OK, I've reconsidered my position. Rocky vs. Tyson—Rocky by 1st round knockout; Rocky vs. Frazier—Rocky by 1st round knockout; Rocky vs. Ali—Rocky by 1st round knockout; Rocky vs. Godzilla—Rocky by 2nd round knockout. I know—*how* could Godzilla get him into the second round? Well, I happen to know, Godzilla has a really good chin." They laughed and I went back to praising Todd Foster. All was forgiven.

When I do the shows at a Las Vegas location like Mandalay Bay, we know what to expect. But, when I take it on the road to smaller riverboat or Native American casinos, sometimes I have to improvise. Once I went to a small casino in Colorado and they were so anxious to get me up there that they did not exactly tell the truth about their facilities. There was no lounge or showroom as they suggested. There was a tiny makeshift stage in the middle of the casino with a sound system that makes my son's karaoke look impressive. I couldn't play the video clips that are such an integral part of the show—there was no video screen. I had to have them rig up my CD player so I could at least have the background music for some of the songs in the show. I am adventurous, but even I had some serious doubts. I suggested that based on all this I wasn't sure I should try and do a show, and I chastised the general manager for being just a smidge less than honest. Then I saw that the casino was filled with people surrounding this stage. They had been advertising all week and there were about seven hundred people jammed into a casino floor that was not made for that many. I couldn't call it off at that point.

I wasn't even sure they would all hear me with this "state of the art" sound system. I mumbled to myself, "Oh what the hell," climbed up on the stage, and took a whack at it. Luckily I had told the casino executive that under these circumstances he better give me a *lot* of prizes to give away for trivia questions. I was thinking I might have to buy their affection with prizes. With slot machine bells going off around me, no room to move, and a stage that seemed destined to collapse, I just kept asking trivia questions, mixing in some sports songs that I hoped they could hear, and doing the longest and wackiest Q&A period ever. I managed to survive, and somehow this sardine-packed crowd of boxing fans was happy.

One fellow was playing a slot machine next to this low stage. He was so close to me he was practically a cast member of the show, and yet he *never once* looked at me or acknowledged that I was entertaining seven hundred people right next to him. At the end of the show, after the applause for my closing musical number, I said, "I want to thank all of you for coming, but there is one man I especially want to thank. Without him I could never have done this show," I turned and put my left hand on the shoulder of my *still* slots-playing and oblivious friend and said to the crowd, "A big round of applause for my partner Fred." As they were laughing, right on cue, he finally looked up from the slot machine he was playing, turned around, and waved to the crowd. A standing ovation for playing slots. Now *that* is talent.

These Boxing Party shows serve many purposes for me. One is that I truly do get a chance to hear firsthand what boxing fans are thinking about. It is not good to exist in a vacuum without fan reaction. During the shows I often ask a poll question about something having to do with boxing, get a vote, and then give the audience a chance to voice their opinions.

After the shows, I get a real chance to chat with many of the audience members, and I love connecting with the people who are keeping me on the air by supporting boxing on television. Ninety-nine percent of the people I meet are good-natured and fun. For my comrades in television who don't want to break that fourth wall I say, "Do it, it's fun."

I have even performed this show from a boxing ring. Once at an Iowa state fair I was making an appearance at a boxing match and they asked if I could do an abbreviated version of my show from the ring before the fights started. After the last story, you now know that inside a ring was a piece of cake compared to other venues. After the fights that night, the general manager of the building gave me a note. It said, "Al: Love your boxing commentary. I enjoyed your show tonight—it was a lot of fun. And, I liked your music . . . Best wishes, Kenny Rogers." The general manager of the building told me that Kenny had performed the night before at the state fair and decided to stay for the fights the next night. He was incognito at the event, but passed along that lovely note. If I had known he was there I could have asked him a trivia question. I'm sure he could have used one of the baseball caps we were giving away as prizes.

I morphed my night club music act into an interactive music, video, trivia show known as The Boxing Party. I have taken it all over the United States and internationally in my never ending effort to "break the fourth wall." It has produced moments that were fun, interesting and challenging.

In the show we often have models who serve as hostesses to go around and bring the microphone to folks who want to ask me a question, or they give the prizes to winners of trivia questions. Normally these are attractive and classy young ladies. A few years ago at a casino in the Midwest, the crowd was reacting in a much more animated way than normal when someone answered a trivia question correctly. It appears that every time that happened, one of the young ladies working with me would celebrate by pulling her top down. Apparently the entertainment director had hired them from a local topless club, and no one bothered to tell them that this was a bit more G-rated. I caught on when I saw some horrified faces mixed in with the happy ones. I looked back just in time to see one of these young lovelies with her top down. With the morals clause of my Showtime contract flashing before my eyes, I marched over to her, put my arm around her, and said, "I guess they didn't tell you, only I go topless in this show." Having accomplished my mission of getting a laugh, I remembered that morals clause again and whispered in her ear, "If you and your friend stop doing that now, I will double what they are paying you." She winked and nodded her head. From that point on they were very well-behaved. And, I learned again how dangerous it could be to go out there and break the fourth wall.

Less Is More

A book called *Those Guys Have All the Fun—Inside the World of ESPN*, was released in May of 2011. Although it does not say "literary critic" on my business card, I still felt the need to write and deliver a commentary about this highly anticipated book. Here is the special commentary/book review that I did on The Boxing Channel in June of 2011:

"Most of you know that I spent almost twenty-four years as a sportscaster at ESPN before moving over to Showtime in 2003. I made my debut on ESPN about six months after it launched. So, I had a long role in the evolution of ESPN from fledgling cable network to multimedia powerhouse. Along with my colleagues, I lived this story.

Now comes what many suggest will be the definitive book on the ESPN journey. It is an oral history gathered by two presumably prestigious authors. One did an oral history on Saturday Night Live and the other has been a longtime television critic at a major newspaper. Oral histories have a rich tradition in literature. You get to hear firsthand from participants in the story being told in an oral history. The great Chicago author, Studs Terkel, refined this art form with several oral history books during his long career. The one he did on the Great Depression in the United States remains a literary masterpiece.

The keys to making an oral history work are good editing of your subjects' interviews and good transitional prose by the author to tie the interviews together and advance the story lines. This book on ESPN has none of that. The two men who put this book together either didn't believe in editing, or were too lazy to do it. Instead, they produced seven hundred pages of largely unfiltered comments filled with hubris and ego by those giving the oral history. This is a book that sinks under its own weight.

While there is some cogent commentary and a few juicy nuggets that will titillate some ESPN devotees, this book does little to inform about the fascinating process of building and maintaining ESPN. I was a firsthand witness to and participant in that remarkable journey for two-and-a-half decades.

The writers were content to lead their interview subjects to the water of self-aggrandizement and colleague bashing, and most were quite willing to drink from these fountains. The book is filled with shameless spin doctoring in which most everyone was intent on showing that they were right about things that their former and even current colleagues got wrong. This is a book about settling scores, a book about getting even, and a book about puffed-up squabbles among the well known and not so well known.

What this book is not, is a well-told story about one of the most amazing media success stories in history. ESPN's success came with personal dramas that included everything imaginable. There were mistakes that almost brought the dream to an end, then brilliant creativity that saved the day, often when ESPN's funding was not unlimited. I would have liked a coherent and lean approach to telling that story instead of the ponderous and leaden manuscript that they did produce. In the end, this book did provide a few fun and salacious tidbits that will give us all a chuckle. Is that really enough to get for the thirty dollars you will shell out to buy this seven-hundred-page turkey? I think the answer is no."

As you may have already guessed from chapters about ESPN in this book, the story of that network's development has many layers to it. Because of the nature of my book, and because telling ESPN's full story is not my mission statement here, I have focused mostly on the whimsical and humorous parts of that evolutionary tale. Call me a nut, but I figured you would like to be entertained and informed with some interesting and funny events in ESPN's history rather than reading windy, self-important pontification of behind-the-scenes feuds and ego battles. If you really want that, well, you can buy that other book, which I might point out is a lot more expensive than this one.

Blessed Are the Storytellers

The story of Ray Mancini is more than remarkable. The telling of that story to the world is something that fell on the shoulders of two of my closest associates in broadcasting. One told his story as it happened, and the other relived it for a new generation years later. In both cases they did so superbly.

My regard for Ray could not be higher, as our lives intersected in intriguing ways. I too participated in much of the storytelling of Ray's fascinating career. It is ironic that Ray is now a movie producer, because he lived a life that could have been fashioned from the pen of a great fiction writer. But, his story is quite real, and it needs no embellishment.

As a young boy growing up in the 1960s, he sequestered himself in the basement of his family's house in Youngstown, Ohio, to look at newspaper clippings of his father Lenny's boxing career. As a lightweight contender, Lenny battled Sammy Angott to a standstill in 1941. A world title shot hung in the balance, and Angott received a split-decision win. Angott would go on to win the world title in his next fight. While a Mancini title shot was being negotiated, World War II intervened. Lenny went off to war, and two years later returned with a career-changing injury. He was never able to get a title shot.

Young Ray read the clipping of his dad's exploits and vowed he would make the title dream become a reality for the Mancini family. He dedicated himself to boxing, and after a brief but explosive amateur career, he turned pro in 1979 and moved from the then economically depressed former steel mill town of Youngstown to the bright lights of New York. When he was sixteen wins into his pro career, his older brother, Lenny Jr., was killed in an accidental shooting back in Youngstown. It was a gut-wrenching time for Ray and his family. This event would begin at amazing seventeen-month period in which he would have more highs and lows than most people face in a lifetime.

I met Ray a few months after this tragedy, when he was fighting Al Ford on the *Top Rank Boxing* series in April of 1981. I had only been on the air at ESPN for maybe nine months. I was green as a sportscaster, but even I could tell Ray was ticketed for stardom. A comic sidelight to this is that heayweight contender Duane Bobick was also doing color commentary on this fight, and he got a little too caught up in the moment. At one point he put his headsets in his hand, jumped up, and started yelling encouragement and instructions to Ray. Not exactly your objective analyst at ringside. I remember the producer saying, "Where is that screaming coming from?"

As I was having my first experience with Ray, it turns out he was also getting to know someone else. Ray often attended the shows of an up-and-coming show business act known as the Rocco sisters, and Ray became a friend and frequent racquetball-playing partner with Connie Rocco. The very same Connie Rocco I would meet thirteen years later and marry fourteen years later. Over the next several years I too became friends with Ray and could easily have met Connie then through him. But that was not to be.

Six months and two big wins later, Ray was fighting for the lightweight title against Alexis Argüello. Here he was living out his father's dream of fighting for a world title, and against a legend no less. That afternoon, with millions watching on CBS, he fought as well as anyone could for a little over ten rounds. Then he wilted a bit and Arguello was able to get to him in the 14th. It was a stirring fight, and Ray's stock rose in losing. America was getting to know Ray Mancini, and they liked him.

Here is where David Dinkins Jr. enters the picture. David, who is now the executive producer of Showtime Sports, was a young producer for CBS back then. He did one of the first features that told America the Mancini story. David said, "The story was so compelling. You had Ray coming from a working-class family, fighting for a higher purpose, carrying on the family name in boxing. He was trying to rectify the bad break his father got, while still getting over his brother's death. As a piece of fiction it would have been over the top. People asked me all the time if the story was manufactured. It wasn't. This was the real Rocky story with many more layers. Sylvester Stallone was not Rocky, but Ray Mancini was Ray Mancini."

David was producing the live show on CBS in May of 1982 when Ray challenged again for a lightweight title, this time against Arturo Frias. Frias rocked Ray in the first round and then it became a wild slugfest. Ray won by 1st round TKO. His father's dream had been fulfilled by his youngest son, less than a year after the death of his oldest son. The seemingly down-and-out city of Youngstown, Ohio, had something to cheer about. Ray couldn't miraculously change the economic status of his hometown, but he could give its residents something to feel good about.

David, who was a neighbor of Ray in Manhattan at the time, remembers something about Ray that is important: "He never got caught up with all this and got carried away with himself. And he was becoming a big star."

With a brilliant manager in David Wolfe and all of America invested in his story, the future looked boundless for Ray. Wolfe was a well-known author who wrote the book *Foul*. This story of basketball player Connie Hawkins remains perhaps the best sports book ever written. Dinkins remembers Wolfe: "I was a big fan of the book *Foul*, and he was a fellow New Yorker. We had a good relationship. I would say that without David, Ray might not have become the star he did. Yes, Ray had to be ready and do the fighting, but Wolfe maximized his potential."

Then came November 13, 1982. That was the day that Ray fought Duk-Koo Kim, a mandatory challenger from South Korea. It was thought to be an easy title defense for Ray. It was anything but that. The twenty-three-year-old Kim had a 17–1–1 record coming in, but no one knew if he could fight. He walked out in the opening seconds and blasted Ray with a left hand. Ray would say later, "That was it, I got hit with that first big shot and it was on." Was it ever. Over thirteen-and-a-half brutal rounds they waged a classic war. Finally the tide turned and Ray knocked him out in the 14th. It had been a war of attrition, and Kim was carried out on a stretcher.

Later that night it became known that Kim was in a coma and the prognosis was not good. "The fight was overshadowed by the tragedy," Dinkins points out. He adds, "It was a great fight that would have been remembered for that, if not for the tragedy." Indeed, it turned into a tragedy when Kim died.

The morning after the fight David got an exclusive interview with Ray, largely on the strength of their relationship. That interview aired on CBS News that night. A fight that had a star-studded live audience, watched by millions in the afternoon on CBS, had become a nightmare for Ray, for Kim and his family, and for boxing. "It was terrible," David remembers, "It's surreal to read about history, but to live it and be right in the middle of it is very different. That was a tough interview to do."

"I was at his home in Youngstown when we did features, and of course I saw him in New York all the time. I was personally invested," David said. I don't know how families deal with their relatives in the ring or now in the cage [for MMA]."

To add even more irony to this, Ray's trainer Murphy Griffith was the brother of Emile Griffith, who had seen Benny "Kid" Paret die after he knocked him out in 1962. And, Gil Clancy, who was announcing the fight for CBS, had been Emile's trainer. These men had to relive that all over again.

For Ray it was a devastating thing to deal with. Within a seventeen-month period his brother had been killed, he had failed and then succeeded to win a world title, he became a popular figure in America, and then he saw an opponent die days after a brutal battle. Hard to comprehend all of that happening in such a short period. Ray's resiliency made it possible for him to go back in the ring only three months later, beating George Feeney by decision.

I re-entered the picture seven months later when I announced the pay-per-view telecast of Ray's fight with Orlando Romero. Ray had some trouble with the left handed style of Romero (foreshadowing of what was to come), but he stopped Romero in the 9th.

When Ray defended his title for the seventh time against Livingston Bramble, it was being syndicated on stations around the country, and I was working the telecast with New York sportscasting icon Bill Mazer. Bramble was a decided underdog coming into the fight, but he made the prefight period an unpleasant one by taunting Ray as a "killer" and doing everything possible to get under Ray's skin.

As a sports television producer David Dinkins Jr. has few peers. He is a master at telling stories as they are happening. No live sports television producer does it like David. One of those stories he told expertly was the amazing journey of Ray "Boom Boom" Mancini. David has been a valued colleague and, more importantly, one of the best friends I've ever had. (Photo by Pearsi Bastiany/Impact Photos)

There was a packed house at Memorial Auditorium, virtually all Mancini fans. Ray was doing very well into the 4th round when Bramble switched to lefty. The problems that Ray had had before with lefties cropped up again. It was the game changer in this fight. Still, after twelve rounds Ray was ahead on the scorecards, but back then title fights were fifteen rounds. Ray ran out of steam and was stopped in the 14th. I remember doing the postfight interview with David Wolfe in the ring. Again Ray's world was rocked with another surprise. Wolfe was heartbroken. The subsequent rematch with Bramble was as close as could be, and Bramble squeaked out a decision win. Ray would never challenge again for the world title.

In the intervening years I would work with a talented producer named Craig Mortali, who worked on the *Sportscenter* coverage of big fights. Craig's true calling came when he moved to ESPN Classic to do documentaries. The culmination of his documentary work with Classic came in 2007, when ESPN Classic was shutting down its original programming department. That to me was a sad moment. I had participated in many of the Classic shows over the years.

For Craig it was painful because his love and passion was in that genre of programming. He was asked to do the last of the major documentaries to be done by Classic. It was to air on the twenty-fifth anniversary of the Mancini-Kim fight. The show was called *Triumph and Tragedy*. Craig said, "I was determined to make the best show I ever produced. I was going to hit a home run with this."

The subject matter was close to Craig's heart. "I have been a boxing fan all my life, and we covered some of the greatest moments in the sport's history for *Sportscenter*. I loved the texture of Ray's family and the way they endured hardship. He is Italian, so am I. We are about the same age. Everything about this hit home to me."

While the Kim tragedy was the reason for doing it, Craig fashioned a show that was about much more than just one tragic night. It told the story of the Mancini journey with pathos and accuracy. It also made us understand the anguish of the Kim family and his South Korean friends.

The layers to this story seem never ending, and the show dealt with two poignant stories related to that tragic afternoon in 1982. The referee for that fight, Richard Green, would commit suicide months after the fight—many feel because he was haunted by the fact that Kim died on his watch, though no one who viewed the fight blames Green for what happened. And Kim's mother also committed suicide not long after her son died, anguished over the loss of a son and family squabbling over his $20,000 purse from the fight and a $5,000 death benefit.

Triumph and Tragedy is simply the best sports documentary I have ever seen. I urge everyone to get a copy of it and watch it. I was happy to be one of the participants in the show, which brought me full circle with Ray.

You might think that a story as rich and dramatic as Ray's would not require great storytelling. That's not the case. The story itself is so compelling that the storytellers can't intrude on it. They need to tell it simply and accurately and let it breathe. That is exactly what David Dinkins Jr. did when it was happening, and what Craig Mortali did twenty-five years later. They both did Ray Mancini and his story complete justice. I am proud to call all three of them friends.

A postscript to this story comes several years ago when my wife Connie and I reached out to Ray to help us for The Caring Place, the facility my wife co-founded to help those touched by cancer. We needed him to come to Las Vegas as a celebrity for a Dancing With The Stars Benefit Night. As you would expect from Ray, he jumped right in to help his friends. He rehearsed the dance for weeks in Los Angeles, came to Las Vegas, and dazzled the crowd. And, of course, he won. Once a champ, always a champ.

You Never Know
Where You Will Find Excellence

Without boxers there would be no boxing. That may seem like the most painfully obvious statement I have made in this book. I can assure you, however, that sometimes the people who run the sport seem to forget that fact.

If boxers are the lifeblood of the sport, then that would make trainers the nutrients that keep the blood flowing and efficient. Trainers are the second most essential people in boxing. They are also the most fascinating people in the sport and the best talkers. They usually express a passionate vision of what their fighters can do, and they are often willing to comment honestly (and sometimes provocatively) on other things going on in the sport.

Trainers are a varied lot, as diverse as any group could be. There is no telling where you will encounter a good (or even a great) one.

In the mid 1980s one of our frequent stops for the ESPN show was the Reseda Country Club in Los Angeles, California. The featured fighter was often slick boxing middleweight Michael Nunn, who was trained by Joe Goossen and promoted by Ten Goose Boxing. Joe's brother Dan ran Ten Goose, and the two of them are part of an amazing family made up of eight brothers and two sisters. Their dad was a Los Angeles police detective, and his character is best summed up by this story that Dan tells: "For my first promotion my dad came up to me and said he wanted me to charge him for his tickets. I told him I couldn't do that. He insisted. He said that everyone would be asking me for free tickets, and if I could tell them that he was charged for tickets, then they would know they could be charged."

For ten years Ten Goose did monthly shows from Reseda, and it was a great atmosphere. It was an intimate room filled with fans—often famous ones. Celebrities flocked to the fights there. When we did an ESPN show there I would sometimes go into the audience and interview the likes of George Wendt, Gene Hackman, David Hasselhoff, Billy D. Williams, Sylvester Stallone, and others. It was great fun.

In the midst of all this I got to see Joe Goossen work. Joe had never been a boxer, yet he was able to become a superb trainer. No one in the sport is more tireless in working in the gym with a fighter to create and perfect a winning game plan. No detail is too small for Joe. On fight night his instructions have specificity and urgency, but they are never frenzied or confusing.

Joe is also good at training to a fighter's strengths, not his own preferences. He molded Nunn into perhaps the best pure boxer of the last thirty years. Then he took two brothers, Gabe and Rafael Ruelas, to world titles. They had very different styles than Nunn. Along the way Joe has worked with a number of champions including Joel Casamayor and Diego Corrales.

Joe was at the center of one of the most interesting stories I've chronicled during my time at Showtime. He had been the longtime trainer of two-division champion Joel Casamayor. Joe had trained Casamayor in a thrilling TKO win over Corrales. Then they parted ways, but in the very next fight Corrales asked Joe to train *him* for his rematch with Casamayor. Awkward. Joe was in Corrales' corner for this rematch. This was unprecedented. It was not an easy situation and Joe handled it with great diplomacy. Corrales had lost due to cuts in the first slugfest. In the rematch Joe had Corrales box more, not brawl, and he was very effective winning a decision.

There is one other thing. Joe is funny—really funny. If Joe can't make you laugh, then you do not have a sense of humor. And I am not talking about slapstick, lowbrow humor. Joe's humor is clever, even erudite. It's just a fact—Joe Goossen is the Noël Coward of boxing!

Given that, it's not surprising he has done some work as a television boxing commentator, and I hope he does more. He is an excellent ringside analyst, and I would love to call some fights with him some day. As friends watching fights he and I have approximated that, but not on television. With more opportunities Joe could make a name for himself as a commentator.

Did I say boxing commentator? That brings us to Emanuel Steward. From sunny California we move to Detroit, the place Manny put back on the boxing map with the Kronk gym in the late 1970s and '80s. The ESPN series made stops in Detroit in the early '80s to do matches with the second-tier fighters from Kronk—men like Bill "Caveman" Lee, Micky Goodwin, and Dujuan Johnson. Those men produced exciting fights that added to the Kronk legend. The Caveman Lee-John LoCicero match (see chapter 12) was a classic.

One of the highlights of those trips to Detroit was going to the fighter meetings, where we could get information for the broadcast. It was like auditing a class with a great guest lecturer when Manny Steward talked at those meetings. But he wasn't lecturing. In fact, he wasn't even making himself the center of attention. That belonged to his fighter. He was simply answering questions posed to him and occasionally interjecting nuggets of boxing knowledge where necessary.

Earlier in this book I compared Manny to Gil Clancy. There is no higher praise for me to bestow. Manny has trained so many champions that it's easier to name the ones he has *not* worked with. In one of the more amazing feats he has trained a heavyweight champion for almost two decades straight. First Lennox Lewis had his long run as champ (with two small interruptions), and then came Wladimir Klitschko.

Manny is class personified. He exudes class. He has the kind of smooth demeanor that we all wish we had most of the time. He has it 100 percent of the time. Everyone wants to spend time with him—it's always fun. And you can always count on him for support. He has never failed to attend fundraisers for The Caring Place, the nonprofit facility my wife co-founded for those touched by cancer. He never hesitates to help.

One of his finest moments came in the ring after Lennox Lewis defeated Mike Tyson. Leading up to that fight Tyson's behavior had been over the top, even for Tyson. He attacked Lewis at the press conference announcing the fight and even bit his leg. The comments Tyson made denigrating Lewis and his corner were harsh by any standards. With all that, Manny consoled Tyson in the ring after he lost to Lewis. In front of the television cameras he thanked him for all the thrills he had given to all boxing fans. It took character and compassion for Manny to do that.

Already a member of the International Boxing Hall of Fame, Manny adds to his legacy every time he works a corner or does a boxing broadcast. My friend Jerry Lewis calls Manny a "treasure" for boxing fans. That description works for me.

There are world-class trainers who get to train champions, like the two men previously mentioned. Then there are world class trainers who, through no fault of their own, don't have champions on their resumes. Such a man is Phil Daley, who can be found in Lake Charles, Louisiana. It's probable that neither the man nor the place resonate with you. Neither is famous.

My first visit to Lake Charles took place in 1982 when the ESPN boxing series went there to feature up-and-coming welterweight star Donald Curry against homegrown product Mike Senegal. Phil was the promoter and also the manager/trainer of Senegal. The night of January 13, 1982, produced two things I had never seen. The first came when Senegal was cut and the ring doctor was called in to look at the cut. He not only looked at the cut, he administered to it for at least thirty seconds, then our shotgun microphones clearly picked up sound of the good doctor giving Senegal some advice on fighting. Before he sent him back to the action he also gave Senegal a brief pep talk! Not exactly an objective ringside physician. By the time the action resumed Sal Marciano and I were dumfounded and said so on the telecast, but that was nothing compared to what was to follow.

There had been rumors that Curry had the flu and might not be 100 percent. And so, when a big cut emerged in one of his gloves in round 5 it raised some suspicions. Was this a ploy to give him a rest? There was a five-minute delay while they got the gloves and they were laced on Curry's hands. Then it happened again in the same round, again a delay. Then in round 9 it happened *again*. Sal said on the broadcast, "What are the odds of this happening?" Indeed.

Another delay ensued and Curry seemed renewed enough to finish Senegal off. He would stop Senegal in the 10th round. The Curry camp claimed the glove tearing happened because there was some sharp edge on Senegal's mouthpiece. Some were skeptical of that theory.

That Lake Charles excursion gave us highlight reel material for every ESPN boxing anniversary show thereafter. It gave me something more—a lifelong friendship. The day before the fight I went with Phil out to his home on the outskirts of Lake Charles in the even smaller town of Ragley. His lovely wife Darla cooked the best pork chops I have ever eaten. To paraphrase the girl in the movie *Jerry Maguire*, Phil had me at pork chops.

The ESPN boxing series would return several times to Lake Charles, and I personally would return there dozens of times not just for more pork chops, but also because it became a second home to me, and Phil became like a brother.

Don't think for a moment that my friendship with Phil clouds what I am about to tell you. I think you know me better than that. When it comes to dispensing boxing opinion or analysis I have never played favorites. Friend or not, Phil Daley is one of the best boxing trainers I have ever seen. With a talent pool much less plentiful than exists in the big urban centers of our country, he has produced a dozen or more solid professional fighters who *all* were made infinitely better by Phil. Every fighter Phil sent out there on national television knew how to fight. You can't teach the sport any better than Phil does. He has not found his world champion yet, but that does not diminish his skill set or achievements with boxers.

Around the world there are coaches in every sport who make athletes better, and they are the men and women that matter most to me, whatever level their athletes reach. Athletics is about getting better and performing to your highest level. Yes, winning is somewhere in the equation, but if we trivialize those first two goals, then we cheapen the idea of sport.

I can think of dozens of boxers on every level that I watched improve every time out. I urged viewers to celebrate that. I often qualified that with the statement that the fighter may never become a champion. The important thing is to acknowledge and enjoy that smaller moment of triumph. I know that Joe Goossen, Emanuel Steward, and Phil Daley would agree with that statement. That's really the essence of being a good boxing trainer. These three men come from different areas, different backgrounds, and even different cultures. What they share is the passion and ability to make boxing the sweet science. They do it one person at a time, and that's what's most important in the sport.

Revisiting History
Is Enlightening and Fun
(PART 2)

Is it cheating for me to use the same undeniable truth twice in this book? Does it show a lack of creativity on my part? Does this compromise the title of my book? Why am I asking so many questions?

OK, here's the truth (as opposed to what I have been feeding you for twenty-four chapters). After I finished with this undeniable truth the first time, I looked at some of the commentaries I did on boxing history for ESPN that I did *not* include in that chapter. And I was sad . . . for you. How could I, in good conscience, deprive you of more of those commentaries, especially knowing how much you must have loved them earlier in the book?

Then, a day or two later, I was up late watching ESPN Classic, and what do you think I saw? Right—how did you guess? It was one of the commentaries I did that was *not* in that first chapter. Well, naturally I took that as a sign from above, a divine intervention that I should include more of those commentaries in this book.

So, it became apparent to me that the only reason to repeat this undeniable truth was to selflessly serve you the reader. Well, that and the fact that the alternative chapter left me about fifteen hundred words short for the book. But, mostly it was the first reason.

All that silliness aside, the first of these essays/commentaries I present here will demonstrate why I wanted to share some more of these with you—especially this first one. Ironically, it is not about boxing. ESPN Classic was doing a special thirtieth anniversary presentation of the movie *Brian's Song*, with other special features on its story. I was delighted to be asked to open that show. Here is the essay I delivered that night:

BRIAN'S SONG

Every city has its defining sports heroes and stories. For those of us who will always call ourselves Chicagoans, no matter where we are living, Gale Sayers is one of those heroes, and his friendship with Brian Piccolo is one of those stories.

When these two men met at the Bears training camp in 1966, the NFL was just beginning to change into the big business monolith it is today. The Bears were one of the last vestiges of the old ways, a family-owned team actually coached by the owner himself—George Hales.

All Chicago fans were excited back then about our Bears. After all, the 1963 championship was still fresh in our minds, and the team had added Dick Butkus and Gale Sayers to the roster. And, Sayers had delivered an astonishing rookie year in 1965. It was a time of unbounded optimism.

But, only three-and-a-half years later Gale Sayer's greatness was lost to injuries, his good friend and teammate Brian Piccolo was dead from cancer, and it seemed that everything had changed. Grief and unanswered promise had replaced optimism. In many ways the 1971 movie *Brian's Song*, chronicling these times, helped heal the wounds. The film was done so beautifully that it gave us all some kind of needed catharsis. And, the movie diffused the pain a bit by truly making this an American tragedy, not just an emotional burden we Chicagoans had to bear. It also did something else. It reminded us not only of Gale Sayer's greatness and Brian Piccolo's spirit, but also how much friendship and courage really matter.

(As a postscript to this essay, I received more reaction to this short appearance than any other single thing I have ever done on television. The highlight of that reaction came in the form of letters and e-mails from several

good friends of Brian Piccolo. They thanked me for expressing these sentiments and for setting the stage for the airing of a movie that would inform another generation about this remarkable story.)

Here are some more remarkable stories. These are from boxing's rich history.

MATTHEW SAAD MUHAMMAD

The word "warrior" is often overused in the world of sports, but rest assured it can be used in connection with former light heavyweight champion Matthew Saad Muhammad. With an iron will forged from a childhood in which he needed one, Muhammad rose to the top in boxing while fighting in a light heavyweight division that might have had the deepest talent pool in the history of the sport.

Orphaned as a child, he and his brother had a nomadic childhood that included shelters and reform schools in Philadelphia. Through it all Matthew kept his resolve, and when he saw Muhammad Ali sparring in a Philadelphia gym he knew boxing was his calling. He attacked the sport with a fervor and zeal that made him one of the most admired fighters of this great era.

He won the title in one of the best light heavyweight matches ever held. He and then-champ Marvin Johnson engaged in a bloody and exciting battle that finally ended in the 8th, when the fight was on the verge of being stopped because of cuts over both of Matthew's eyes. Over the next two-and-a-half years, he would defend his title eight times—all exciting fights.

Muhammad fought at a time when all of the top light heavyweights were not just good, but excellent. He fought virtually all of them before or after he won the title. Men like Eddie Mustafa Muhammad, Mate Parlov, Yaqui Lopez, John Conteh, Richie Kates, Dwight Braxton, and Johnson made up an impressive list of the fighters he battled. He had two wars each with Johnson and Lopez.

From the mid 1970s through the 1980s the light heavyweight division was magnificent, and Matthew Saad Muhammad played a major role in making it so. For that he is in the International Boxing Hall of Fame, and for that we will always remember him as a talented and gallant warrior.

ROBERTO DURAN (LIGHTWEIGHT YEARS)

The life and career of Roberto Duran is a play with many acts. The end of act one was in 1972 when a young, svelte, and mean-spirited Duran invaded New York City to challenge for the lightweight title against a very good champion, Ken Buchanan. He would batter Buchanan to win the title. When historians talk of the impact of Duran as a great fighter, it is usually the lightweight Duran that they speak of in reverent terms. That is the Duran that they place high on the list of great boxers in the sport's history. Duran was a dominant force at 135 pounds, holding the lightweight title for five-and-a-half years while defending it twelve times. Remarkably, in between those title defenses he won twenty-one nontitle fights, losing just one.

The Duran of that era was quick, powerful, and relentless. He never gave opponents room to breathe, and yet he was already perfecting the good defensive skills that would really surface in many of his later fights. He controlled a division that was hardly bereft of good fighters. He had to beat good boxers to hang onto the title, and perhaps the best was Esteban DeJesus, the only lightweight to beat Duran. That win came in a nontitle fight, but Duran destroyed him in the rematch, with the title on the line.

If some of the later incarnations of Duran at higher weights appeared to tarnish his lightweight legacy, well, they shouldn't. A viewing of any of his lightweight title fights will remind you just how great Roberto Duran was at 135 pounds.

RUBIN "HURRICANE" CARTER

The story of Rubin "Hurricane" Carter's life is as dramatic and compelling as any you will ever see. That's why it was the topic of a major motion picture and a popular Bob Dylan song. Because of all that, some people have suggested that Carter was one of the great boxers of his era. Others counteract what they perceive as show business mythmaking by denigrating Carter's skills. The truth about Hurricane Carter, "the Boxer," lies somewhere in between those extremes.

Before he was unjustifiably sent to prison for murder, ending his boxing career, Carter was a very good middleweight. He was one of the best of the early 1960s. He was powerful and ferocious in the ring, a reflection of his demeanor at that time outside it. Despite all his talent, with the exception of his 1st round knockout of welterweight champion Emile Griffith in a nontitle fight, Carter was seldom able to get the job done in career defining fights. He did fight for the world title against Joey Giardello, and when Giardello was able to withstand Carter's big bombs early in the fight, Carter lost confidence and the champion came back to win the decision. In fact, against top fighters like Luis Rodriguez, Dick Tiger, and Joey Archer, Carter was winless. However, in his run up to a title shot from 1961 to 1964, he was an exciting fighter who left thoroughly beaten opponents in his wake.

So, when we think of Rubin Carter, "the Man," we see someone who conquered injustice and his own personal demons. When we look at Hurricane Carter, "the Boxer," we see a fighter who couldn't quite conquer the middleweight division. But he came darn close and created a lot of excitement in the process.

OSCAR BONAVENA

Oscar Bonavena was an Argentine heavyweight contender who lived his life in the fast lane and died the same way. He was also a man who helped define the heavyweight division in the late 1960s and '70s, even though he never won a world title.

For a man who liked to party a little more than he liked to train, Bonavena still used his toughness and strength to bedevil top heavyweights—principally the two giants of the era, Joe Frazier and Muhammad Ali.

Oscar would fight Frazier twice. On the first occasion, in 1966, it was the twenty-two-year-old Frazier's coming-out party at Madison Square Garden. The Olympic champion was undefeated as a pro and ticketed for greatness, but Bonavena sent him to the canvas twice in the 1st round. Joe came back to pound out a tough ten-round decision, but later said that hitting Bonavena was like hitting cement. Two years later they fought for Frazier's heavyweight title. After fifteen brutal rounds, Frazier had another decision win. Joe often said that Bonavena was one of the toughest men he ever faced.

Ali's battle with the tough Argentine in 1970 was Ali's second fight back after his three-year boxing exile, and only months before he was set to fight Frazier in their first big match. But Bonavena was giving Ali huge trouble all through the match. Frazier, sitting at ringside, told his manager Yank Durham, "Ali's gonna blow our payday." He wanted to rush Ali's corner and tell *him* that. In the 15th round Ali landed a punch from nowhere that dropped Bonavena. It was the only time anyone ever stopped him.

Oscar's carousing caught up with him at age thirty-four when he was killed in connection with a love affair he was having with the wife of a Nevada brothel owner. His lifestyle cut his life short, just as it helped short-circuit his boxing career. Still, he will always be remembered as the man who more than tested two boxing legends.

ARCHIE MOORE

The facts about Archie Moore are remarkable. His twenty-seven-year boxing career spanned seven presidential administrations. He knocked out 141 opponents, more than anyone in boxing history. He won the light heavyweight title at age thirty-nine and held onto it for six years— twice fighting for the heavyweight title. He battled seven men who, like him, are enshrined in the Boxing Hall of Fame.

Amazingly, all those athletic achievements seem almost insignificant when you compare Archie Moore, "the Fighter," to Archie Moore, "the Human Being." Archie was a true renaissance man, a self-educated person who appreciated literature and philosophy as much as others appreciated his boxing skills. He developed a positive, but not naïve, approach to life that allowed him to play through the disappointment of being a top middleweight and light heavyweight contender for almost twelve years before finally getting a title opportunity at the age of thirty-nine.

Was he passed up for title shots because, as some historians suggest, there was some sort of quota for black champions allowed in boxing? Or was it simply that The Old Mongoose was too good for anyone to risk their title against? Either way, he was frozen out, but he persevered and ultimately the prize was his.

Archie's life is best summed up by the name of the youth organization ABC—Any Body Can, which has been carried on by his son, Billy, after his death. As an elder statesman Archie was a sage and sometimes eccentric philosopher. He remains the most interesting athlete I have ever met, and I'm not sure there is even a close second.

CARMEN BASILIO

From 1948 to 1961, the span of Carmen Basilio's career, there were probably more great active boxers in all weight divisions than any time before or since. That he is included in those ranks speaks volumes about this tough battler.

Carmen was called The Onion Farmer because he grew up on such a farm in upstate New York. He would give that nickname worldwide recognition, making it stand for toughness, courage, and excellence. What kind of fighter was he? If you look in the dictionary next to the word "aggressive," it ought to show Basilio's picture. Backward was not in his vocabulary.

In his tremendous career he won the welterweight and middleweight crowns, fought five future Hall of Famers, and had two exciting wins with almost—Hall of Famer Tony DeMarco. Those are two of the best fights of this great era.

The signature night of Basilio's career came on September 23, 1957, when he stepped up in weight to challenge the middleweight champ Sugar Ray Robinson. That night they produced fifteen rounds of total fury—a fight that is on every single top ten greatest fights list. Basilio won the fight and the world title. The late, great Chicago raconteur Ben Bentley, who was present for everything that mattered in sports for five decades, was the ring announcer that night. In the twilight of his years Ben told me that this fight was the most special sports event he had ever attended.

I am not a memorabilia collector, but years ago I was given an original press packet from the Basilio-Robinson fight. I am told that it is perhaps the only one still in existence. The only person who will ever get it from me is my two-year-old son Wes when he grows up and I can tell him all about the great Sugar Ray and the man they called The Onion Farmer.

(As previously noted in this book, the boy who was two years old when I wrote that commentary is now twelve. He is not the biggest boxing fan in the world, but he more than understands why this item is important in terms of history, and why it is important to me on a personal level. This summer, when I am inducted into the International Boxing Hall of Fame, Wes will meet The Onion Farmer who, along with my idol Sugar Ray Robinson, created one of the most special moments in sports history. That quaint-looking press packet sits in my office as a constant reminder of what those men did.)

The Rear Naked Choke Hold
Is Here to Stay

One of the more remarkable marketing successes of the last twenty-five years has been the selling of mixed martial arts, and more specifically the UFC, to the world. This is a sport that is in such an embryonic state that it is still defining itself, and yet it has already become a big part of the pop culture of America and indeed the world.

I know that to some of the people reading this book that last paragraph probably made them grimace. For a certain number of boxing fans, MMA is objectionable. They see it as some kind of unskilled street fight. They see two fighters who don't throw punches that well, resorting to elbowing, kicking, and hitting their opponents when they are already down. They consider two men rolling around on the mat looking for submission holds as boring and somewhat odd.

I don't share that opinion of MMA. And some have suggested that on the occasions when I have hosted and done play-by-play on MMA shows, I have somehow become a "turncoat" on boxing. Here's one such posting from a viewer:

"Al I was so surprised to see that you announced mixed martial arts. You are a Jedi who went to the dark side. I can't believe that you like that sport. Please don't help them destroy boxing."

Wow. I knew that there were tensions between the two sports, stoked by ill-informed people within both sports and the media. Still, I never thought that by accepting a couple of assignments to do MMA I would go from being a Jedi Knight to a Sith Lord. I showed this posting to my twelve-year-old son, a *Star Wars* scholar, and he said, "Oh my gosh, Daddy, this means you are Count Dooku!" OK, that's it, I am outraged, and this MMA-Boxing feud has gone far enough. We must bring peace to the galaxy! If you are not conversant with *Star Wars*, (referred to in our house as "The Gospel according to George Lucas"), you will just have to Google Count Dooku to better understand. I don't have time to explain, I have a galaxy to save.

The only way to bring peace to these dueling cultures is to debunk the myths that have been perpetuated about boxing and MMA. As Yoda himself once said, "Cloud our judgment the dark side does." (OK, I promise that is the last *Star Wars* analogy in this chapter, but if you had to Google Yoda, you are beyond help.) So, let's go myth debunking.

MYTH I—An MMA match is just two guys in Speedos engaged in a street fight with a crowd watching.

Years ago I was asked by the UFC to do a show—really almost an infomercial for the sport of mixed martial arts. Back then they actually needed a well-known boxing figure to add credibility to the show. I said yes to it even though I was not knowledgeable about mixed martial arts. Actually, that was the reason I did say yes. I was curious to find out more. I was, I believe, convincing in reading the script and hosting this show. In truth, however, I had no idea what I was talking about at least 50 percent of the time. If I did that same show now, I would at least be conversant enough in MMA language and concepts to do a better job.

That show made me somewhat more understanding of MMA as a sport, but I remained a casual fan until 2007 when I was asked by Showtime to fill in and host one of the *EliteXC Challenger* shows. In advance of that show I studied hours and hours of videos of matches and devoured written material about MMA. That studying, and discussions with Stephen Quadros, the expert analyst on the show, made me start to understand that MMA is a nuanced and challenging sport.

To be a great mixed martial artist you have to be great at minimally one or two of the different disciplines and at least passable in several more. For instance, even if you are not an expert at initiating jujitsu moves, you must at least be adept at avoiding them. MMA is, in fact, a more complex sport than boxing when performed correctly.

I have hosted about a half dozen MMA shows in recent years, and I have always been careful to make sure that I do not overstep my boundaries and offer opinions or be an armchair expert. Being a boxing analyst does not make you an MMA analyst . . . not even close. I have called matches with some very knowledgeable people including my Showtime colleagues Stephen Quadros and Pat Miletich, as well as Phil Baroni. And, I've been on Showtime year-end wrap-up shows discussing MMA with Frank Shamrock and Mauro Ranallo. I have tried to listen carefully to all these talented analysts and drink in what knowledge I can. Announcing these MMA shows has been an absolute joy, made better by the talented analysts who share the microphone with me. I hope to do more in the future.

My firsthand broadcasting experiences and simply listening as a fan have taught me that MMA is complex and interesting. The ground game that some people denigrate as "boring" is in fact fascinating when it is explained properly and you watch it carefully. In one of the matches I announced on Showtime, one of the fighters was dominating the first two rounds. Then right at the end of round 2 the other fighter got him into an armbar with seconds remaining in the round. It was exciting to watch the seconds tick down to see whether the trapped fighter could make it to the end of the round or would have to tap out. He tapped out with just five seconds left in the round. That was as exciting as any knockout I have called as a boxing announcer.

MYTH 2—MMA fans are not boxing fans, and boxing fans are not MMA fans.

This is one of those myths that the media has helped perpetuate, and to some degree some of the people involved in these sports have as well. It is generally accepted that MMA's demographic is younger than boxing. I am sure that's true, though probably not to the degree that some would have us believe. And, does that premise take into account the people who like both sports?

I have been fortunate that my forays into mixed martial arts announcing have been made with brilliant analysts at my side. Here I was teamed with the "Fight Professor" Stephen Quadros (left) and MMA legend Pat Miletich for a Strikeforce show on Showtime. It was one of the most enjoyable broadcasting experiences I've had. (Photo by Tom Casino/SHOWTIME)

While this is unscientific, I would use me as a good measuring stick. In doing MMA shows and being around the people involved with MMA, I have found that there are many crossover fans. Many mixed martial artists have boxing backgrounds as well and will always love the sport of boxing, even though they participate in MMA. And, among the MMA experts, *all* of the ones I have met like boxing. The announcers I previously mentioned are all big boxing fans as well. I assure you the number of people who like both sports is *much* larger than the common perception.

Even Dana White is a boxing fan, though some think otherwise. He started out in the sport, and even his bashing of the boxing hierarchy does not diminish that. I have a theory about Dana's attacks on boxing figures. I would make the analogy to Muhammad Ali's needling of Joe Frazier. With Ali, at first it was designed to hype their fights and perhaps gain some kind of psychological edge. As time wore on it took on a life of its own. It had the sharp edge of cruelty, and it did collateral damage to Joe in the black community. Ali was friends with Joe at one point and had respect for him, but at some point Ali could not figure out how to dial down the needling. He had almost created a public relations trap for himself and couldn't get out.

I actually believe the same has happened to Dana. He started needling boxing as a way to elevate his sport, by defining what he perceived as things that made the MMA model better than boxing. The backlash from boxing folks, who also probably had their own agendas for doing so, only escalated Dana's assaults. It appeared as if Dana were declaring war on boxing, and many in the media assumed that war meant that one of UFC's goals was to diminish boxing and usurp its role in the world of sports. I don't believe that was Dana White's intention because I know he really likes the sport of boxing. I think he, like Ali, is now trapped in a paradigm that is hard to escape. And Dana is an emotional guy who shoots from the hip, so each time he's asked by a media member about a boxing issue, he will comment. The collateral damage to boxing from all this is an unintended consequence.

While some boxing promoters engage in the back and forth with White, many boxing fans have embraced MMA as an interesting sport. One of these groups is the younger Hispanic community, already big boxing fans but courted by MMA and now interested in both sports. The boxing fans I talk to at airports, in hotel lobbies, and at boxing matches who say they like MMA as well are not *defecting* to MMA, they are adding it to their sports menu. This brings us directly to the next myth.

MYTH 3—MMA and boxing cannot both be successful.

Until about two years ago the one topic I was sure to be asked about when guesting on a sports talk radio show was Mike Tyson, even well after he was out of the sport. Now the question I am frequently asked is some variation of this: "MMA is so popular now that it's taking over from boxing—what do you think of that?" To be asked that question in that manner tells me immediately that this particular host is lazy and one dimensional in his or her approach to sports broadcasting. They have heard some form of this bromide repeated often, and like a political ideologue hearing a campaign stump speech, they just assume it's true. And, we know from those stump speeches that just because something is repeated often does not make it true.

There is plenty of room under the contact sports tent for both boxing and MMA. Each has its own fan base and enough people who like both to support both sports quite well. Common sense tells us that. Boxing will not become extinct because MMA is on the scene. There are millions of rabid boxing fans in the United Kingdom with the love of boxing passed down for several generations. Will they disappear because MMA is here? There are millions of Filipino fans that came to boxing for Manny Pacquiao and now love it. Will they evaporate due to MMA? How could boxing ever go away in Mexico and Puerto Rico, where the sport is embedded in the national psyche? In Canada boxing is on the upswing in both Quebec and Ontario, even as MMA also surges in popularity.

In the United States boxing is most certainly more of a niche sport than thirty years ago, but the point is that it has found its niche. That includes millions of fans. All this despite the fact that the mainstream media has shunned coverage of the sport, even in a time when exciting matches dot the boxing landscape. For uninformed and lazy media members it's easy to dismiss boxing as a dying sport, done in by the new kid on the block—MMA. That is simply not the case.

I would make the argument that the rise in popularity of MMA has actually helped boxing. MMA is a very edgy sport—much more so than boxing. MMA has gained a level of acceptance in some quarters where even its zealots might have doubted it would happen this soon. This aids boxing because it has made boxing's tame violence by comparison seem more than acceptable. As a sports personality identified by my association with boxing, I can tell you that over the last thirty years there have been times when boxing's violent nature kept me from certain opportunities. Not so anymore. I have watched the MMA boon lessen the stigma put on boxing.

My message to those running these two sports is simple: Turn down the volume of rhetoric when you talk about the "other" sport. There is no real reason for people representing either sport to denigrate the other one. Any short-term advantages of that (if there are any) could backfire in the future.

My message to the media is also simple: Do your job. Check into generalizations before you mindlessly repeat them.

My goal here is not to coerce fans to like both sports if they truly don't like one or the other. That involves personal taste, and everyone has the right to make their own choice. But I am here to tell everyone that MMA is not going away, as some thought in its beginnings. And boxing is not going away either, as some have begun to think recently. So, it behooves fans, media, and participants of each sport to at least appreciate the other for what it means to its fans.

If a certain sixty-year-old sportscaster, more than thirty years into a boxing announcing career, can do that, then anyone can. Peace in the contact sports galaxy may depend on it.

If You Win the Super Six Tournament, You Must Be Super

The Super Six World Boxing Classic was an interesting and grand boxing experiment. You can't call it an overwhelming success, but you certainly can't call it a failure. You could call it long. It started on April 25, 2009, and did not end until December 17, 2011. It was a bit like a big epic costume drama in the movies that runs about twenty minutes too long, but creates so much compelling drama that you forgive that and sit through it anyway.

The tourney was the creation of Ken Hershman who was in the midst of a very successful six-year run as president of Showtime Sports. Enlisting the aid of five disparate promoters, Ken launched this round-robin tourney. It featured three European fighters and three Americans. It was global in nature and grand in scope. Once it started, to paraphrase Dorothy in The Wizard of Oz, people came and went pretty quickly. Along the way three fighters and one promoter exited. Even Ken left Showtime before the tourney ended. He went to HBO to head their sports division.

There were countless fight-delaying injuries, and surprisingly the tourney did not produce as many action-packed fights as expected. With all that it sounds like the Titanic. Well, it wasn't. The tourney achieved several of its goals: it brought attention to a talent-rich 168-pound division, bridged the gap a bit between U.S. and European boxing, and created a potential superstar. It is the last item that I will concern myself with in this chapter.

When the tournament started, Andre Ward was a 25–1 underdog to win the tourney, but many boxing insiders were picking him to win. This 2004 Olympic champion had been brought along slowly as a pro. Some thought that was because he had deficiencies. Only a win against veteran Edison Miranda stood as a notable win on his resume. But still, those in the know whispered that he was the one to watch in the Super Six.

The coronation started in his first fight when he took on the tourney favorite, Denmark's Mikkel Kessler. I never thought that Andre would dominate Kessler completely and bully him in the process. He did just that. Notice had been served. Andre just kept winning. He beat Allan Green, Arthur Abraham, and then the charismatic and talented Carl Froch in the final.

Along the way Andre never came close to losing a fight. With this window to the world he just kept getting better and better. The Super Six anointed a star and it was Andre Ward.

And yet, there is a fly in the ointment. Most sports fans say they want athletes to be solid citizens that their kids can look up to. They bemoan the behavior of petulant, self-centered athletes whose behavior is often inappropriate. Then when an athlete emerges that does meet their criteria for a role model, they don't find him (or her) spicy enough to merit attention.

Andre might be such an athlete. He is now one of the four or five best boxers in the world. Someday soon he may be the best. Outside of the ring he is intelligent, well spoken, and forthright. He is a spiritual man who does not hide his religious beliefs, but does not try to impose them on others.

In my more than thirty years of announcing I've interviewed thousands of boxers, and many have been impressive men both inside and outside the ring. As the total package I can say without hesitation that Andre is the most impressive boxer I have ever met. The combination of excellence inside the ring and outside it is a bit surreal.

Don't misread this. Even with his strong religious beliefs and straight arrow attitude about life, Andre Ward is not anyone to be tampered with. This is where sports fans should see nuance instead of stereotypes. Andre is a tough, tough man. He physically manhandles opponents inside the ring (sometimes even bending the rules), and brooks no foolishness outside it. With a vocabulary and a delivery that is pitch-perfect, he can make the boldest of points at a press conference without it seeming like bravado. In fact, it is just that. No one is more confident than Andre, and no one is more competitive. He hasn't lost a fight since his early teens.

With all that, however, comes a delightful and respectful man. He treats his wife and children with obvious love and respect, does not upstage those around him, and still manages to seize opportunities to advance the Andre Ward brand. That's a combination of behavior that is almost impossible to pull off.

He wants to be more than a boxer, yet he never takes shortcuts as a boxer. He has already started a broadcasting career and shows the same attention to detail to that as he does boxing. His work as a boxing analyst for NBC at the 2012 Olympics is a springboard for him in the broadcasting profession. I have shared a microphone with him on several occasions, both at ringside and covering a fight. He is a sponge who drinks in knowledge and lets nothing go unnoticed. In less than ten years he will be the best boxing analyst on the planet. And that's with this pesky boxing career getting in the way.

As to that career, there is a light heavyweight title in his future when he is done with the 168-pound division. He has a good five-year run in him as a great fighter. Amazingly he insists he's still a work in progress. If that's true, that's bad news for anyone between 168 and 175 pounds. A better version of Andre Ward is a bit scary.

As you may have guessed from chapter 16, I am not an authority on anyone's theology. Yet one cannot ignore Andre's nickname, which is The Son of God. Only he could have *that* nickname and explain matter of factly that it doesn't mean he is *the* Son of God. He says that name can apply to all who are Christians. And that seems like a plausible thought even to the uninitiated like me. I bring this up only to point out that even this potential land mine in our combative society does not explode for Andre. The reason it does not explode is because Andre is not using his religion as a marketing tool. He proudly displays it because that's who he is as a person. It goes no further. He will never get the blowback that a Tim Tebow gets because Andre's faith it seems is designed to be internalized to make him a better person and athlete. I am not attacking Tebow. I'm simply making an observation.

If you spend ten minutes with Andre Ward and you do not come away impressed, then you are either jealous or obtuse. In a sport that is often defined by bad behavior and overstatement, Andre refuses to engage in either. We will see if most boxing fans can appreciate that or not. They should. He's super; it says so right in the name of the title he won. That's good enough for me.

The World Boxing Classic Super Six trophy sat next to host Gus Johnson during one of the Super Six telecasts on Showtime. That trophy went to an extraordinary fighter and man, Andre Ward. If the Super Six was sometimes imperfect as a tourney, it crowned a winner who seems to have few imperfections. (Photo by Pearsi Bastiany/ Impact Photos)

I Tweet Therefore I Am

It has recently become evident to me that life without Twitter would be a dull and meaningless existence. With the exception of the DVR and deep-dish pizza, it is the greatest invention ever. An overstatement you say? I think not. If you are on Twitter you know everything two seconds after it happens, you can provide information to thousands of people without a filter, and you will always know when a Kardashian is eating a meal, driving in a car, or just had an argument. I rest my case.

The social media is now the most effective tool for anyone to get their message across to large groups of people without going through a media gatekeeper. That's why I was put on Twitter in the first place. You can convey information as you see fit, as long as it doesn't take more than 140 characters. Some suggest that Twitter further dumb us down in our communication skills. Absurd. My response: OMG I am LOL at that, b/c tweeps communicate gr8.

The goal on Twitter is to get a large number of followers. I'm doing pretty well. I have about seventeen thousand followers, which puts me only six million behind Paris Hilton. But then, her tweets are riveting—here are the last four:

> At airport to go to Australia
> Here we go, taking off . . .
> Took a nap, OMG we have WI-FI on plane!
> Hello Sydney, I'm here.

Now *that* is storytelling, I feel like I took the journey with her.

I have to admit I am uneasy about the designation of people as followers. When I think of someone having followers I think of dictators or cult leaders. Although, I may be worrying needlessly because followers on Twitter don't exactly go along mindlessly, Even though I am paid to be a boxing analyst, you'd be amazed how stupid some of my tweets on boxing have been. I know this because some of my followers have pointed this out to me. Sometimes they point it out in a pretty forceful way, with words that don't need an abbreviation on Twitter.

For a noncombative person like me, you would think things like that would turn me off to Twitter. No sir. For every one of those people there are scores of others who are as nice as can be. Entire relationships are built on Twitter. I think I may have inadvertently married someone from Scotland last week. I hope my wife won't be angry.

I try to stay on message and talk about boxing, sports, and things my management reminds me to promote. But it's hard to do that. Twitter is seductive when it comes to going off topic. Some find it charming when I digress to topics like the theater, movies, or current events. Others use those expletives that need no abbreviation. And what if some really fascinating person tweets you on another topic? How do you not respond? I think that's how I ended up with a Scottish bride.

It could be I am addicted to Twitter. In fact, my goal is to pass Paris Hilton in followers. You can help. Get everyone you know to follow me @Albernstein. I promise not to disappoint you. Here is a sample of the great tweets to come:

Sitting ringside for fight
OMG, spilled my drink
5th round coming up
OMG, pen out of ink
Fight's over
OMG, broke my reading glasses
Back @ hotel
OMG, tweet from Scotland!

Gene Kelly Said It Best:
Every Partner Brings with Them
Something Special and Unique

If I am going to "borrow" an undeniable truth from anyone for this book, I'm not ashamed that it's the great dancer, Gene Kelly. He may have been the most talented man who ever walked the earth, and he was smart too. That doesn't seem fair does it? Well, anyway, his quote about dance partners applies to most any kind of collaborative relationship, and certainly to sportscasting. I have worked with a long list of creative and talented partners at ringside, and each did bring something unique to the mix.

Since I have served as both an analyst and play-by-play announcer in boxing, I have announced fights with virtually every broadcaster who has done the sport in the last thirty years or so. I've compiled what I think is a complete list of those broadcasters, and it is quite eclectic. It includes scores of iconic play-by-play broadcasters, champion boxers, actors, trainers, a referee, two former NFL players, one former major league baseball player, a volleyball great, and two brothers. There are announcers from the United States, Canada, Great Britain, and Ireland. Here, in no particular order, are the folks who have put up with me at ringside as a broadcast mate.

Steve Albert, Gil Clancy, Steve Farhood. Tom Kelly, Dave

Bontempo, Raul Marquez, Sean O'Grady, Barry Tompkins, Gus Johnson, Howard Davis, Sal Marchiano, Barry McGuigan, Bob Papa, Gerry Cooney, Antonio Tarver, Mario Lopez, Roger Twibell, Nick Charles, Dave Farrar, Ray Mancini, Steve Grad, Arda Ocal, Bob Sheridan, Bill Mazer, Tommy Hearns, Maureen O'Shea, Hawk Harrelson, Mr. T, Rich Marotta, Len Berman,, Charley Steiner, Benny Ricardo, Andre Ward, Tony Page, Jim Simpson, Jesse Reid, Joe Mesi, Brian Viloria, Sam Rosen, Dave Roberts, James Smith, George Foreman, Ben Bentley, Bob Trumpy, Corey Erdman, Chris Marlowe, Don Chevrier, Al Michaels, Bob Ley, Sam Smith, Bernardo Osuna, Tom Treiber, Bert Sugar, Marv Albert, Fran Charles, and Joel Meyers.

I never even expected to meet half the people on this list, let alone work with them. And this list does not include the men and women reporters and hosts I worked with at *Sportscenter* on ESPN, or the MMA announcers I referenced in the last chapter who worked with me on that sport. Add to them the analysts I worked with when doing play-by-play on college basketball at ESPN, and it's quite a group.

The longest continuous partnership I have had was with Barry Tompkins. In 1988 he came to ESPN to do college basketball, football, and boxing. For a little over seven years we did more than forty shows a year together, crisscrossing the country and doing shows at locales that ranged from outdoors at a cow pasture in Gardnerville, Nevada, to the Blue Horizon in Philadelphia. To understand the nature of the Blue Horizon you need only know that it was adjacent to a crack house. Barry captured the essence of this venerable old boxing club at the top of the show when he said, "Tonight we welcome you to the Blue Horizon in Philadelphia, a place that reeks with boxing history . . . actually it just reeks."

Another frequent location was the Showboat Hotel in Las Vegas, a property that was also a bit long in the tooth. The boxing was fun there, but we hated having to stay at that hotel. Barry fixed that. During one telecast we were bantering a bit and Barry channeled his inner vaudevillian and said, "My room here is so small the flies have to walk." I laughed, but the Showboat management didn't. I can thank Barry for many things, one is getting us out of the Showboat. As a postscript to this, only two months later I was on a plane going from Los Angeles to New York, and sitting next to me on the cross-country trip was the president of the Showboat Hotel. It was a frosty five hours.

In between punch lines, Barry also did a great job of calling the fights, as he does calling so many other sports. Now we are teammates again at Showtime.

The second longest-running collaboration for me has been with Steve Albert. That was for six-and-a-half years starting in 2003. When I left ESPN to go to Showtime it was a special move for me. I was going to be able to call meaningful matches with top-notch production values attached to the show. Getting to team with Steve was an added bonus. Steve is part of the first family of sportscasting. His brothers Marv and Al, and his nephew Kenny, are all well-known announcers. Steve, of course, is the best looking and most talented one in the family. (Steve, did I say that the way I was instructed?)

Steve did an ESPN show in the early 1980s with me in Texas, and he made me laugh when he introduced us as the suburban cowboys. Then we didn't work together for almost twenty years. Actually, I think he had a clause in his contract forbidding it. No, he welcomed me graciously when I joined *Showtime Championship Boxing*, and I found out that in addition to being perhaps the nicest sportscaster anywhere, he is also the best prepared. His notes for fights are legendary. On my first Showtime show Jim Gray pulled a prank on Steve and hid his notes at ringside. It was an interesting few minutes for Steve, to say the least.

I felt Steve's pain because at the 1986 Marvin Hagler-John Mugabi match, someone did take all my notes from ringside, and I did not get them back for the show. I had to re-create them as best I could in twenty minutes. It was not an easy night. Then after the show a man came up for an autograph and I realized I was about to sign *my notes*! He was trying to hide it so I'd sign the top and not see the contents. He had taken them so he could have a nice souvenir from a big fight, and then had the nerve to ask me to sign them! I wanted to slug him, but there were people all around waiting for signatures, including some kids. It's the only time I ever refused an autograph. Wait, there was that one process server . . . but that's another story.

The two men I have worked with the longest, though not

continuously, are Dave Bontempo and Steve Farhood. For a while in the mid 1980s Dave worked with me on the *Top Rank* series. For the fights on the East Coast I did play-by-play with Dave as the analyst, and for the fights out west the very talented Tom Kelly did play-by-play and I was the analyst. Even though sometimes I was on the verge of an identity crisis, the joy of working with Dave and Tom made it a fun time. Dave has been a great friend ever since, and he is as talented a boxing announcer as you'll find, both as analyst and play-by-play voice. We now get to work together covering boxing at the Boxing Channel (www.boxingchannel.tv), and he does his usual excellent job. Dave has a photographic memory, so he doesn't even need those pesky notes at ringside. He just remembers everything. Heck, he can recite lyrics to me from song parodies I did at a musical show he attended more than twenty years ago. I can barely remember one word from the song.

In the early 1980s, in only my second foray doing play-by-play on the ESPN series, I was teamed with Steve Farhood. Already a well-respected boxing writer, Steve was beginning his sportscasting career in that period. Since that time, I have had the pleasure of working with Steve many times on pay-per-view events and on the *ShoBox* series at Showtime. He too now adds great commentary to the Boxing Channel. Steve has imprinted the *ShoBox* series with his personality and knowledge, and whenever I am assigned to do one of the *ShoBox* shows it's a special treat because I get to work with him. Keep that between us, though. If Steve hears that he'll get a swelled head.

I value consistency of performance more than almost anything, and few can match Bob Papa when it comes to that. I worked with Bob for several years on the ESPN boxing series, and I can tell you he *never* makes a mistake . . . *never*. His broadcasting mechanics are amazingly good. His work on NFL broadcasts and boxing on HBO has continued to raise his profile, and he deserves this success.

I said few can match Bob's consistency . . . well, one who can is another New York based sportscaster named Sam Rosen. Sam was on the first ESPN show I ever worked on in 1980, and he and I worked together a lot in those early days. He dubbed us The Bagel Boys and also gave me the nickname Prince of Pugilism. As the longtime voice of the Rangers hockey team, Sam is a New York icon, just as Bob Papa is becoming with his work with the Giants. Bob, Sam, Steve, and Barry as well, are so adept at guiding the broadcasting ship so you never worry about capsizing. I have loved doing play-by-play over the years, and I'm still hoping to leave a telecast where I feel that it all went perfectly. Judging from their work, these men should leave almost every telecast with that feeling.

Speaking of New York icons, it's time to mention my first regular partner, Sal Marchiano. People in that city looked to him for their sports news on television for decades, and I was privileged to work with him right at the beginning of my career. In 1980 Sal was brought to ESPN as its signature sportscaster. He was a major figure in the sports world and he was friends with everyone from Joe Namath to Jack Nicholson.

As for me, well, I was, how shall I put this . . . nothing. Really, I had written a little book on boxing and had done a few shows on ESPN as an analyst, and I was just then getting a chance to really prove myself. There was no reason for Sal to be deferential in any way to me, but he was exactly that. He treated me as a broadcast equal, allowed me the space to grow on the air, and helped me do it. For that I will always be grateful. Off the air he and I and *Top Rank Boxing* Coordinator Akbar Muhammad became the three musketeers, galloping around the country doing these shows and having more fun than it seemed possible.

I was actually in awe of Sal. One day he was casually telling me about playing golf with James Garner. He told me that "Jim" wanted to convey to me how much he enjoyed us on the boxing telecasts. I said, "Wait, James Garner knows who I am?" Sal laughed and said, "Well you are on television, and if he's watching me, he's watching you too." OK, that was logical, but somehow it still didn't seem plausible to me.

My collaboration on Showtime with Gus Johnson and Antonio Tarver has been a good one. Gus injects enthusiasm and excitement into the call of the fight. Antonio has already become the best boxer-turned-commentator we've seen in many years.

Perhaps this photo with Showtime colleagues Steve Albert and Antonio Tarver tells you all you need to know about the experiences I've had working with my many broadcasting partners. With few exceptions, it has all been this much fun. (Photo by Tom Casino/SHOWTIME)

While I'm sharing names of those I worked with in front of the camera, there are many behind the camera that make all broadcasts special. I have mentioned some of the producers and directors I've worked with already in this book. I can add names like Ken Dennis and Gary Clem who did the ESPN *Top Rank Boxing* series with me and Barry Tompkins for more than seven years. They are very talented, and more importantly we all share the same sense of humor. Being on the road together for fifty shows a year requires that.

Ray Smaltz, an excellent producer, who does many of the *Showtime Championship Boxing* shows, has been a longtime associate and friend. My stints as host of the *ShoBox* series on Showtime have allowed me to work with a special group of people that includes Executive Producer Gordon Hall, Producer Rich Gaughan, and Director Rick Phillips.

As coordinating producer of *Sportscenter* at ESPN, David Brofsky provided me with guidance, opportunities, and friendship. Many of my fondest memories of working at that network involve David.

This brings me to Jody Heaps. Jody merits special attention. Why? Because sportscasters never want to be outdone. I'll explain. Some years ago, former Showtime commentator Ferdie Pacheco devoted almost an entire page of his memoirs to praising Jody. So, naturally, when I began writing this book, I felt the need to give my good friend and colleague Jody equal treatment, lest he go around saying he liked Ferdie more than me. That would never do.

So, I will now tell you about Jody. As creative director for the *Showtime Championship Boxing* series, he creates and/or oversees all those great features you see on the show. He is also executive producer of the highly acclaimed *Fight Camp 360* series. In his spare time he is a talented playwright who has had several of his plays produced in New York and Los Angeles. Oh, I forgot to mention that he is tall, handsome, and irresistible to all women. OK, that last sentence is a bit of a stretch, but I am trying to out do Ferdie here..

Jody also believes he is a boxing expert. He has some very eccentric ideas about the sport. He claims that well over 50 percent of boxers are lefties. I have no idea why he thinks this, but this theory is very important to him. I have tried mightily to explain to Jody why this theory is wrong, even resorting to facts to make my point—to no avail. Jody has a master's degree from Harvard, so you would think he might use his considerable intellect to advance some movement that is just a little more important. But, no, this crusade to enlighten all of us on left-handed boxers is central to Jody's mission statement in life.

So, we are more than two hundred words and four paragraphs into Jody's story, I think he should now like me better than Ferdie. Of course, this could all be temporary. What if there is some other sportscaster out there just waiting to write his or her memoirs, who is willing to give Jody *two* pages of attention? Then he will like *that* sportscaster better than me, and I'll have wasted valuable space in this book that could have been used puffing up someone who could enhance my career. See, being a narcissistic sportscaster is a lot harder than it looks.

I am sure you can still remember the cranky Al in chapter 8 who took many of his colleagues to task for the "me first" approach. Despite that negativity, I love sportscasting and sportscasters. We are like modern day gunslingers, traveling the country and staying ready for the moment of truth when that red light comes on the camera. At that moment we need to draw quickly and shoot straight. Sportscasting is all about delivering when that light comes on.

I won't pretend that everyone on the list at the beginning of this chapter is equal in performance. But everyone on that list, whether neophyte or veteran, brought something unique to the moments I have shared with them on the air. I hope they can say the same about me on their list.

Things Have a Way
of Coming Full Circle

I was once a pioneer. No, this is not my Shirley MacLaine moment. I am not suggesting that in a previous life I was a member of the Lewis and Clark expedition. My pioneering came in the 1980s. Along with my colleagues at ESPN, I was pioneering cable television. Cable was the new frontier for sports programming back then. It led to a revolution in how sports programming is delivered to the masses. Now, more than thirty years later, I find myself pioneering again. The World Wide Web has become that new frontier. I joined the fray in 2010 when I became executive producer of the Boxing Channel, which finds its home at www.boxingchannel.tv.

There had never been a channel devoted entirely to boxing before, though many have been suggested. The Boxing Channel fills that need with coverage of matches, features, live boxing matches, and a great library of historical fights. One of the intriguing things about distributing it over the Internet is that there are no other gatekeepers. There are no TV stations to pigeonhole the programming or mess with its placement. There are no cable companies to put your channel on a tier that prohibits viewership. The mandate given to me was simple: create something worth watching and then help tell people to come and watch. The simplicity of the idea is delicious . . . one I could not pass up.

Maybe it seems odd to some that at this point in my career I would want to pioneer something new. It shouldn't. When it was announced that I was to be inducted into the International Boxing Hall of Fame, that announcement seemed like a beginning to me, not an ending point. Yes, it validated my past endeavors in a profound way that I would never have imagined happening. But it also served to energize me to serve the sport that has given me so much, and push the boundaries of delivering sports.

I want to help the sport service its existing fans and reach out to new ones. The best way to do that is with coverage that doesn't compromise fairness just because the Internet provides no external gatekeepers. Others may choose to go that route; the Boxing Channel does not. Channel Coordinator Laura Alvarado, a talented young woman, has helped me set up a channel in which gate keeping of our product is done from within. There is no room for bias, mean-spirited, or misinformed coverage. On the Boxing Channel there is plenty of opinion and color, provided mostly by the sport's participants. Our hosts provide responsible and well-informed opinions as well, but as I said in chapter 8, analysis and fact form the basis of those opinions. Toward that end I turned to talented contemporaries like Steve Farhood and Dave Bontempo to help me provide this commentary and reporting. We have also added young and talented journalists like Marcos Villegas and Crystina Poncher, who are at the beginning of their exciting career journeys. They deserve their chance to pioneer.

Now that I am down to my last few paragraphs in this book, I find myself asking some important, almost philosophical questions:

Why didn't I save myself a lot of work and call this book *30 Years, 20 Undeniable Truths About Boxing, Sports, and TV*? Did I include enough *Star Wars* and political references to impress Jon Stewart, so I can get on *The Daily Show*? Is it insecure to worry that you will like Jeremy Schaap's excellent afterword better than the book that preceded it? Who will play Tim Tomashek when they make this book into a movie?

I am without answers to those pressing questions. But, there is something I do know. Experiences worth having and people worth knowing should both be shared with others. That was my intent in writing this book.

So, while I continue to work at my craft at places like Showtime in the United States and Channel 5 in England, I present to the world the Boxing Channel. It is a unique combination of endeavors. I am excited about the future and the experiences still to come in broadcasting and webcasting. That's how it was for me thirty years ago. Now, so many undeniable truths later, it feels the same.

A career that started out for me pioneering Cable television continues now in pioneering the World Wide Web. Interviews like this one I did with Floyd Mayweather Jr. are part of the Boxing Channel's video programming. Boxing is now an internet based sport and as Executive Producer of the Boxing Channel I am part of delivering boxing programming to fans in this new way.

AFTERWORD

By Jeremy Schaap

Over the last thirty-five years, the world of boxing, as ever, has been populated by giants and pygmies, rogues and renegades, the mild-mannered and the manic. And I'm only talking about the broadcasters.

But seriously.

In the age of Tyson and Mayweather Jr., Pacquiao and Jones, boxing fans became accustomed to craziness, from the spectacle of a man with a fan lashed to his back flying through the Las Vegas night and crashing into the ring as Riddick Bowe and Evander Holyfield were fighting for the world heavyweight championship, to the travesty of a judge scoring the first Holyfield-Lennox Lewis fight for Holyfield, to the embarrassment of a riot breaking out at Madison Square Garden after Andrew Golota, the aptly nicknamed Foul Pole, declined to strike Bowe anywhere *above* the belt.

Then there's Mike Tyson, the embodiment of boxing's age of dysfunction, whose less serious offenses included biting both Holyfield (ear) and Lewis (leg).

Fortunately, throughout this era, there's been one man to make sense of the senseless, to celebrate the worthy, and to call out the unworthy.

I speak of the great Al Bernstein, that constant gentleman and keen analyst, a mustachioed rose among boxing's thorns.

It was Bernstein, of course, who first introduced Tyson to the world, from the arenas of the upper Hudson Valley, back when we could all still hope for a long and prosperous PaxTysona. Then, long after it became clear that reality would not conform to our wishes, Bernstein would still be there, in Memphis, in 2002, when Lewis fashioned a brutal end to the Tyson ring cycle. (Tyson's subsequent fights against the likes of Danny Williams and Kevin "The Clones Colossus" McBride don't count.)

Amidst the madness, Bernstein can always be counted upon to calmly and coolly assess the situation. A big man with a big voice, he has never needed to shout—the hallmark of a true pro. Nor does Bernstein feel the need to bash his audience over the head with his vast stores of knowledge. For Al, less is more and silence can sometimes speak volumes. No one has ever accused him of trying to upstage the men wearing the padded gloves. No one has ever accused him of using his public platform to advance his own agenda. No one has ever accused him of playing favorites.

For several years, I was fortunate to work alongside Al as we followed the colorful carnival, the silly circus that is boxing, a sport we both appreciate despite its flaws. Like me, Al believes the best thing about boxing is the boxers, most of whom—even those who become contenders—don't get rich, but usually get damaged. Compared to all other pro athletes, they work harder, risk more, and are rewarded with less. Al knows these truths, and his appreciation of them is conveyed in his analysis. Like comedy, boxing is hard—and Al makes sure his viewers know it.

When someone has been around the fight game as long as Al, you might expect him to become either a hopeless cynic or an inveterate cheerleader. But Al is neither. He still gets excited about big fights— and he still offers pointed criticism. This quality I admire greatly. In our line of work, we must be on constant guard against the temptation to give in to our instincts to overly simplify story lines and personal characterizations. We must, on the contrary, approach everyone and everything from a neutral starting point, informed but not prejudiced by our experiences. That's Al Bernstein, "the Journalist"—smart and fair, solid not flashy.

Then there is Al Bernstein, "the Cabaret Performer," an altogether different kind of presence—the center of attention, a troubadour in a tux. I have seen the show and all I can say is, "Al, you are a man of many gifts."

On that point, there can be no dispute. As a commentator, as a singer, and, yes, as a man, Bernstein wins by knockout

ACKNOWLEDGMENTS

Mary Cummings and the staff at Diversion Books have been a delight to work with during this project. They have been supportive and accommodating in so many ways. Debbie Collins did a superb job copyediting this book, and we thank her for that.

The cover photo for this book was taken by Tom Casino, one of the best sports photographers in the world. In 1991, Tom took a shot at ringside that I used as my promotional picture for years, and then he took this photo, which I also used as my official photo. Both times he captured the essence of me as a sportscaster while shooting at ringside, without special lighting and no time for me to really pose. For lightening to strike twice like that is remarkable. It wasn't luck, it was talent. Tom's skill as a photographer is considerable, but it is exceeded by his warmth as a person. He has my heartfelt thanks.

George Foreman and Jeremy Schaap were my Dream Team as contributors for this book, and they both graciously added their voices. These are two unique and talented people. I will always be grateful for what they did.

This book would never have been completed without the help of Adie Zuckerman, the managing director of Al Bernstein Live. She was an objective and insightful voice during this whole process. Adie also happens to be my sister, so I thank her for a lot more than just her help on this book. Her support in life has been unwavering, and working with her professionally has been a total joy . . . well, except for the times when she pushed me to rewrite things in this book to make them better. Then she was just a nagging sister. Of course, she was always correct in suggesting those rewrites. So I guess that actually made her a smart sister. Big thanks to another member of her household, her husband Jim Dusablon. His computer expertise got us through some tight spots, and he never asked me to rewrite anything.

Finally, I acknowledge my wife, Connie. All through our marriage she has urged me to write a book. As you learned in chapter 15, she is not a person who is easily deterred from any mission. Her encouragement and patience (and my son, Wes', as well), during this process demonstrates again that I am indeed lucky in love.